"This book is absolutely terrific! For anyone wanting a bright and clear primer on the Bible, this is what you've been waiting for. I unreservedly recommend it to anyone with questions about the most important book in history. I'm deeply grateful to my friend David Whitehead for this excellent work."

—Eric Metaxas, *New York Times* bestselling author
of *Bonhoeffer: Pastor, Martyr, Prophet, Spy*

"As a previously cynical, biblically illiterate new follower of Jesus I needed *Making Sense of the Bible* to take me by the hand and lead me through the path of the elaborate complexity and rich coherence of the Christian Scriptures. As a church planter and pastor I am always eager for a well-informed, relevant, and comprehensible resource that I can use to help the unchurched and initiate Christians to make sense of the Bible. As if having a conversation over brunch with a friend, David Whitehead accomplishes this while addressing the common questions and concerns many people have when engaging the Bible."

—Robert Guerrero, New York City church-planting catalyst,
Redeemer City to City

"This is a book that will renew your faith in the God of the Bible. I recommend it for every person who would say that they are on a spiritual journey toward Christ."

—Jon Tyson, church planter in New York City,
catalytic leader of the City Collective,
author of *Rumors of God* and *Sacred Roots*

"*Making Sense of the Bible* will help elevate the relevance of God and show how people can grasp the big concepts of Scripture."

—Dimas Salaberrios, president
of Concerts of Prayer Greater New York

MAKING SENSE

OF THE

BIBLE

HOW TO CONNECT WITH GOD
THROUGH HIS WORD

DAVID WHITEHEAD

BETHANY HOUSE PUBLISHERS
a division of Baker Publishing Group
Minneapolis, Minnesota

© 2014 by David Whitehead

Published by Bethany House Publishers
11400 Hampshire Avenue South
Bloomington, Minnesota 55438
www.bethanyhouse.com

Bethany House Publishers is a division of
Baker Publishing Group, Grand Rapids, Michigan

Printed in the United States of America

Library of Congress Cataloging-in-Publication Data is on file at the Library of Congress, Washington, DC.

ISBN 978-0-7642-1214-7

Unless otherwise noted, Scripture quotations are from The Holy Bible, English Standard Version® (ESV®), copyright © 2001 by Crossway, a publishing ministry of Good News Publishers. Used by permission. All rights reserved. ESV Text Edition: 2007

Scripture quotations marked NIV1984 are taken from the HOLY BIBLE, NEW INTERNATIONAL VERSION®. Copyright © 1973, 1978, 1984 Biblica. Used by permission of Zondervan. All rights reserved.

Scripture quotations marked NIV are from the Holy Bible, New International Version®. NIV®. Copyright © 1973, 1978, 1984, 2011 by Biblica, Inc.™ Used by permission of Zondervan. All rights reserved worldwide. www.zondervan.com

Scripture quotations marked NASB are from the New American Standard Bible®, copyright © 1960, 1962, 1963, 1968,1971, 1972, 1973,1975, 1977, 1995 by The Lockman Foundation. Used by permission.

Scripture quotations marked NLT are from the Holy Bible, New Living Translation, copyright © 1996, 2004, 2007 by Tyndale House Foundation. Used by permission of Tyndale House Publishers, Inc., Carol Stream, Illinois 60188. All rights reserved.

Scripture quotations marked NKJV are from the New King James Version. Copyright © 1982 by Thomas Nelson, Inc. Used by permission. All rights reserved.

Scripture quotations marked KJV are from the King James Version of the Bible.

Scripture quotations marked RSV are from the Revised Standard Version of the Bible, copyright 1952 [2nd edition, 1971] by the Division of Christian Education of the National Council of the Churches of Christ in the United States of America. Used by permission. All rights reserved.

Scripture quotations marked THE MESSAGE are from The Message by Eugene H. Peterson, copyright © 1993, 1994, 1995, 2000, 2001, 2002. Used by permission of NavPress Publishing Group. All rights reserved.

Cover design by LOOK Design Studio

Author is represented by Foundry Literary & Media.

14 15 16 17 18 19 20   7 6 5 4 3 2 1

green press INITIATIVE

To my wife, Kathleen,

*who has remained my inspiration and
friend through the seasons of life.
I could not have done this without you.*

"Blessed are the pure in heart,
for they shall see God"
(Matthew 5:8).

Contents

Acknowledgments

Many people have helped me along the way to creating the book that you now hold in your hands. Stefanie Peters spent hours nurturing and editing my writing skills. Carl Vasser has been the technical engineer behind *The Daily Bible Verse,* causing that humble commentary to be used around the world. Chris Park of Foundry Literary & Media, and Andy McGuire of Bethany House, took a chance on this new, unknown writer. Last but not least, the Community of Grace has given me many wonderful opportunities to test and adjust this material in the bold landscape of New York City.

I am deeply indebted to each of these and many others on this journey. Thank you.

Introduction

All Scripture is breathed out by God and profitable for teaching, for reproof, for correction, and for training in righteousness, that the man of God may be complete, equipped for every good work.

—2 Timothy 3:16-17

The goal in reading the Bible is not to simply *read the Bible.* The goal in reading the Bible is to *get to know and interact with the God of the Bible.*

Sound radical? I stumbled on to this understanding when I first became a Christian, and it has been the way I have approached the Scriptures for more than thirty years. For me, the Scriptures have been a guide in the darkness, a lifeline when I have felt overwhelmed, and much-needed correction when I have overestimated my own spiritual importance.

There are a lot of books about *how to read the Bible,* so why do we need another one? In many ways, this book is an extension of my experience in writing the daily online devotional *The Daily Bible Verse* (www.thedailybibleverse.org), which has taken on a life of its own on the Internet and now reaches many corners of the world. Of course, one of the wonders of the Internet is how it gives us the ability to interact with one another instantly. As I review the comments on my Facebook page and receive personal emails, one of the questions I am often asked is "How can I understand the Bible?" It seems that even the people who have been exposed to the Bible most of their lives don't know what to do with it.

Most people in this country know what the Bible is. It is sold in most bookstores. Many families have Bibles somewhere in their house, even if it's in the attic or other storage space. Bibles are often given as gifts, especially at times of a birth, marriage, or graduation. When I've mentioned the Bible in conversation, I have yet to hear anyone ask, "What is the Bible?"

The Bible fascinates people. Yet when one tries to read it, there is one obvious barrier: the Bible is a big book.

If you start at the beginning, it's interesting enough: the creation, the flood, the nomads, and Egyptian kings. But beyond that, the Bible takes a different tack: laws for eating, building plans, family trees. Suddenly the reader gets bogged down in a lot of things that seem boring and irrelevant to current everyday life. There is much to be gained from these sections of Scripture, but because we don't see the big picture, we can miss what God wants to say to us through the more detailed portions of the Bible.

This presents a problem in an age when people are reading less. A recent survey from the National Endowment for the Arts (NEA) states that nearly half of Americans between the ages of eighteen and twenty-four read no books for pleasure.[1] Yet when Christians talk about growing in a relationship with Jesus Christ, people are told to read their Bible.

But it's a *really* big book! My copy of the Bible has 1,326 pages. When I first looked at a Bible, I was pretty intimidated. My family did not attend church or talk about the Bible much except in vague terms. At a very young age, I determined that all religions were myths, and I turned to atheism as the only reasonable view of the universe.

At the age of twenty, my roommate became a Christian, and I was determined to get him out of his "religious phase." Yet in my attempts to bring him back to what I considered sanity, I found that Christianity had better explanations about life than my own views of the world. I was confounded, and thus began my journey toward God.[2] I wasn't sure what I was getting into, but I became acutely aware that a force I couldn't see with my physical eyes was drawing me to the historical event of Christ's death on the cross and His resurrection. I realized that if I were to make any sense of these claims about Christ, I would have to understand the claims of the Bible.

As a new follower of Jesus Christ, I didn't know the difference between the Old and New Testaments. There was a major fear factor when I started reading Revelation—all of that stuff about beasts coming out of the water and the threat of Antichrist kept me up at night. I was thrilled to know that the Bible was there to help me, but it took a while for me to get up the courage to ask *how* to read the Bible.

Since that time, I have had the privilege of studying the Scriptures at a seminary level at two major institutions. After three decades, the Bible is more alive to me now than ever before.

You will notice that the chapters in this book are not long and the concepts are basic. These concepts, however, were informed by years of study. As these come alive for you, my hope is that this work will serve as an introduction that will get you started and then inspire you to learn more. There is a list of other great resources to take you forward in appendix B.

With that goal in mind, let's look at the Bible itself and why it is so amazing.

Whether you agree with the Bible or not, it is the most influential book ever written. The Bible is still the number-one bestseller of all time, estimated to have sold more than 2.5 billion copies since its printing on the Gutenberg press in 1451.

Two qualities that distinguish the Bible from other books are the number of writers and the number of books. The Bible consists of sixty-six books written by forty-four authors from three continents.

The Bible was written over a fifteen-hundred-year span and its authors range from shepherds to kings, untrained fishermen to scholars. And because the scope of its authorship is so broad, it cannot be assumed to have been written in isolation. Locations for its original writing include dungeons and palaces, desert wildernesses and sophisticated cities.

The original languages in which the Bible was written are Hebrew, Greek, and Aramaic. The genres of writing include historical narrative, poetry, songs, biography, law, prophecy, allegories, and more. The reader of the Bible will find not only instruction, but also drama, romance, comedy, and action.

Yet despite the great variety of authors, languages, and styles, as well as locations in which it was written, the Bible is amazingly unified. It reads as if the writers got together to make sure their books coincided—a human impossibility!

No matter your view of the Bible, it is relatively safe to say that of all the books ever written, the Bible stands unique.

How is this possible?

When given an English-Arabic translation of the New Testament, Mosab Hassan Yousef was fascinated. As the son of one of the founders of the Palestinian resistance group Hamas, Mr. Yousef was steeped in Islam, but he found a difference as he read the Bible: "I found that I was drawn to the grace, love, and humility that Jesus talked about." The more he read, the more he was changed. Mr. Yousef is now a follower of Jesus Christ.

This is one of the assumptions of this book: that the Scripture is what it claims to be—the very words of God. It has stood the test of time and persecution. It has changed the lives of the great and the small, and it can change your life as well.

Maybe you have heard this before: "The Bible is the oldest book in publication whose author is still alive."

The Bible *is* a big book, but it *can* be read and understood. When the Bible is read with a humble heart and an eager mind, transformation can and does occur. This is what the apostle Paul was referring to in 2 Timothy 3:16 when he said Scripture is "breathed out by God." In some mysterious fashion, God uses Scripture to teach, reprove, correct, train, and equip us for life on this earth. The Bible is God's vehicle to reveal to us the good news—otherwise known as the gospel—which is the very power of God.[3]

I want to invite you to join me in learning how to read the Bible. I believe understanding the Bible is the greatest investment of time you will ever make.

David Whitehead
New York City, 2014

CHAPTER 1

Why Are There So Many Translations?

When we submit our lives to what we read in Scripture, we find
that we are not being led to see God in our stories but our stories
in God's. God is the larger context and plot in which our stories
find themselves.

Eugene Peterson

Once we get past the size of the Bible, the next step of this
journey takes us to a local bookstore or website to buy
a Bible. Now we will face another hurdle in understanding the
Bible: choosing a translation.

When we arrive in the appropriate aisle of the bookstore
(or the search results on a website), it quickly becomes apparent that there is not just *one* version of the Bible. If you did a
search on the web for *The Bible,* you would encounter sites like
www.biblegateway.com, which has over one hundred translations available at the click of your mouse.

The King James Version, the New King James Version, the English Standard Version, the New International Version, the New Living Translation, *The Message*—the list goes on and on. So the question we are faced with is "Why are there so many translations, and how do I know which one is the best?"

A brief look at how the Bible was written can help clear up this confusion.

The Bible was originally written in three languages. The Old Testament was written in Hebrew. Half of Daniel and two chapters of Ezra were written in Aramaic, a sister language of Hebrew. The New Testament was written in the common Greek of the day, the forerunner of modern-day Greek.

Thousands of ancient documents containing the Old and New Testament texts have been discovered, making the Bible the most copied and distributed book in ancient history. More than 25,000 ancient manuscripts have been found to date for the New Testament alone. We have so many manuscripts of the Bible with only minor differences between them that we can have great confidence in the accuracy of the Scripture in its original languages.[1]

That's great news if you can read ancient Hebrew, Greek, or Aramaic. But since the vast majority of us can't read or write in those languages, we need translations so that we can read and understand the Bible in our native language.

Three Methods of Translation

Fortunately, there are a lot of men and women who have given their lives to understanding the Bible in its original languages. As these scholars took on the task of translating the Scriptures, they developed a number of approaches. Here are the basic three, though there are some variations within each approach.[2]

Literal. This is an attempt at a word-for-word translation of the original text into English. As a word-for-word translation, the translators assume that you know what all of the references and sayings meant thousands of years ago. The King James Version and the New American Standard Bible are the most popular versions of this approach.

Paraphrase. A paraphrase attempts to connect more with the ideas in the passage than the exact words of the original. This is the opposite of a literal translation, because the translator connects the ancient text with the grammar and idioms of our day. *The Message* and the New Living Bible are the paraphrases that many people currently use.

Dynamic Equivalent. This type of translation is presented as a middle ground between the literal method and the paraphrase method of translation. This approach takes the original words into account, but then looks for accurate equivalents in English. The New International Version is the best known example of this method. The English Standard Version is another dynamic equivalent translation that leans more toward the literal approach.

Challenges to Literal Translations

One might think that the literal approach is the best form of translation, but it's not so clear-cut. Here are a few reasons why: Translations are word for word, therefore, they assume that you know the common references and sayings from the time period that a particular book was written. For example, let's take a look at 1 Peter 1:13 in the King James Version:

> Wherefore gird up the loins of your mind, be sober, and hope to the end for the grace that is to be brought unto you at the revelation of Jesus Christ.

What does "gird up the loins of your mind" mean? This is a literal translation, but the phrase needs to be decoded for us today. Notice how the New International Version 1984 translates this:

> Therefore, prepare your minds for action, be self-controlled, set your hope fully on the grace to be given you when Jesus Christ is revealed.

Since the New International Version is not a word-for-word translation, it attempts to capture the intent of the original document.

Another drawback to literal translations is the use of measurements. Notice the difference between a literal translation and a paraphrase translation of Numbers 15:4.

New American Standard Bible (literal):

> The one who presents his offering shall present to the LORD a grain offering of one-tenth of an ephah of fine flour mixed with one-fourth of a hin of oil.

The Message (paraphrase):

> The one bringing the offering shall present to GOD a Grain-Offering of two quarts of fine flour mixed with a quart of oil.

Which one do you understand better?

But paraphrases can have their problems as well. Let's look at 1 Corinthians 12:1 in the New Living Translation, which is a paraphrase:

> Now, dear brothers and sisters, regarding your question about the special abilities the Spirit gives us. I don't want you to misunderstand this.

Compare that to the more literal English Standard Version:

Now concerning spiritual gifts, brothers, I do not want you to be uninformed.

The difference between "special abilities" and "spiritual gifts" can be perceived very differently. There is also a significant difference between misunderstanding an issue and being uninformed. There is a strong case to be made for the fact that the literal translation is more helpful in this passage.

The main point is that each method has its own strengths and weaknesses. In their wonderful book *How to Read the Bible for All Its Worth*,[3] Douglas Stuart and Gordon Fee present the following chart to help us understand how the most popular translations generally relate to each category:

Literal			Dynamic Equivalent		Paraphrase
KJV	RSV	NRSV	NIV	GNB	*The Message*
NASB	ESV		NAB		TLB
	NKJV				Phillips

KJV—King James Version	NIV—New International Version
NASB—New American Standard Version	NAB—New American Bible
RSV—Revised Standard Version	GNB—Good News Bible
ESV—English Standard Version	TLB—The Living Bible
NKJV—New King James Version	

We have explored at a basic level the question of why so many translations exist. Now we can address the second half of the original question: Which one is best for you?

Two simple questions can help you decide:

Question #1: Which translation is the easiest for you to understand?

If the translation you are currently using is hard to understand, look at some of the other options we have explored. This is important, because reading the Bible should be more than an academic exercise—it should be a life-changing event (more on that in the next chapter). Having a translation that is enjoyable to read is absolutely vital. Many publishers also offer study Bibles that contain explanations of Bible texts written by the very scholars who translated the texts from the original language.

You may discover that using more than one translation enriches your understanding of the Bible. As we have seen, each translation has a different purpose. Using a paraphrase Bible as a secondary translation can open up the understanding of a text in wonderful ways.

This warrants a brief, but important, discussion about the King James Bible. When many people think of the Bible, they think of the King James Version, which celebrated its 400-year anniversary in 2011. The style of King James English has literally shaped both our language and our Western culture. It has lyricism that almost sings the Bible to us. The King James Version also appeals to literary atheists, who enjoy reading the Bible for its sheer elegance.

But there are some limitations to this venerable translation. When the translators created the King James Version in 1611, they were using the available documents of their day. Since that time, thousands of older and more accurate documents have been discovered.[4] Therefore, the recent translations are considered to be more faithful to the original text.

The other aspect to consider is that language is dynamic and not static. That is, language is always changing. The English used in the King James Version is not the English we use today.

The reader is forced to translate the King James as they read. If you were raised with the King James Version, this can be a familiar and therefore comforting way to read the Bible.

But for others, the King James Version may be too difficult to read. Fortunately, in 1982, Thomas Nelson Publishers released the New King James Version. This translation attempts to update the vocabulary of the King James while maintaining the elegant style and beauty of the original. The New King James still uses the source material of the King James Version but also cites some of the differences in newly discovered manuscripts.

Question #2: Which translation is your local church using?

This might be a surprising factor when looking at the right translation, but Jesus calls all of His followers to be a part of the church. Having a translation that is used in a local congregation makes a lot of sense. It empowers the community at large to have a similar vocabulary of the Scripture, and facilitates following along when Scripture is read aloud.

Bibles for Free

The decision over translations may fade in comparison to the cost of buying a Bible. It seems that publishing Bibles costs a lot of money. Just look at how many pages have to be printed! But if the cost of a Bible is too much, there are a number of ways that Bibles can be found cheaply or even completely free.

Many times local churches have Bibles available to give to people who can't afford to buy one. Just ask the pastor or other leader of a local church if they have Bibles for this purpose. For more options, see appendix B.

We will explore in the next chapter another aspect of reading the Bible that is just as vital as the translations we choose: the condition of our heart.

Summary

We need translations of the Bible because most of us don't know Hebrew, Aramaic, or Greek. For some of us, a direct translation is the most relatable, while for others it may be the relevancy of a paraphrase that suits best, but there are plenty of options to help us understand the history, the stories, and the praises of God in our own language. This should empower us to use the translation we understand best and not to judge someone else on the basis of what translation they prefer.

CHAPTER 2

The Heart of the Reader

Watch over your heart with all diligence,
For from it flow the springs of life.

Proverbs 4:23 NASB

There is an account in the twenty-fourth chapter of Luke of two men walking on a road to Emmaus after the death of Jesus. They encounter a stranger who can see that they are clearly upset. He asks them about their distress as he joins them on their journey.

"How could you be in Jerusalem and not know what happened?" asks one of the men. They recount to him the story of Jesus. They speak of the miracles and the teachings, and then they tell of the tragedy of His death.

As Luke's account unfolds, we find that there is more to this stranger than appears. At the end of their encounter, the two travelers' eyes are supernaturally opened and they realize the stranger is Jesus. There is much to be said for how Jesus reveals himself to them by breaking bread at the dinner table, but the men identify another trait that is a giveaway of His true identity.

> Were not our hearts burning within us while he talked with us on the road and opened the Scriptures to us?
>
> Luke 24:32 NIV

God arranged that they would not recognize Jesus at first. But when Jesus opened the Scriptures to them, the witness of the Spirit filled their souls.

Many writers take great pains to describe the disciplines of reading the Bible. It's relatively easy to find a schedule for reading the Bible in a year or devotionals to help us understand what the Scriptures are telling us. (Find a schedule for reading the Bible in a year in appendix A.) All of these things are wonderful tools, but it is appropriate to remind ourselves of the opening statement of this book:

The goal in reading the Bible is not to simply read the Bible. The goal in reading the Bible is to get to know and interact with the God of the Bible.

In other words, the Scriptures were given to us as a way to know God. Knowing Scripture should not be an end in itself. This is important, because we can know a lot of Scripture and still not know Jesus! The apostle John brings this to our attention in vivid detail as Jesus addresses the religious leaders of His day:

> You have your heads in your Bibles constantly because you think you'll find eternal life there. But you miss the forest for the trees. These Scriptures are all about me! And here I am, standing right

26

before you, and you aren't willing to receive from me the life
you say you want.

John 5:39–40 THE MESSAGE

This is very uncomfortable. When we grasp the story that
Scripture tells us, we see that God is seeking a relationship with
His children. He wants to give us hearts that burn with pas-
sion for Him and His Word. How do we know that? From the
Scripture itself:

And thou shalt love the LORD thy God with all thine heart, and
with all thy soul, and with all thy might.

Deuteronomy 6:5 KJV

Then I will give them one heart, and I will put a new spirit within
them, and take the stony heart out of their flesh, and give them
a heart of flesh,

Ezekiel 11:19 NKJV

But the seed in the good soil, these are the ones who have heard
the word in an honest and good heart, and hold it fast, and bear
fruit with perseverance.

Luke 8:15 NASB

The condition of our heart is very important, because our
heart is the filter through which we perceive all of the Scriptures. If our heart is cold and hard toward God, we can read
Scripture all day and not get much from it. If our heart has a
desire to know God, then just one verse can come alive to us
and satisfy our soul.

So a logical question may be: "What is the heart?" The Scripture mentions the heart more than nine hundred times, but it
rarely refers to the actual organ. It defines the heart as the seat
of our emotions,[1] our intellect,[2] and our will.[3] It is that part

27

of our innermost being that propels us through the seasons of life.[4] The heart is a description of the inner person or the true nature of a person.

Let's say that we are getting dressed for work and we realize that our clothes are feeling tight. *Our intellect* tells us that we are gaining weight, a number of *emotions* flow through us when we realize how our clothes are fitting us, and *our will* either resigns itself to this new reality or determines to change our eating habits and exercise more. All of these thoughts and actions flow together so seamlessly that we are hardly aware of the process.

Similarly, when we don't guard our heart we can approach Scripture with *our intellect* fixed on how little time we have to read, and we rush through the passage in front of us. *Our emotions* can be frazzled from the demands of the day; therefore, *our will* sees no reason to focus our attention on what we are reading. Many times this results in a Bible reading experience that seems lifeless and sometimes frustrating.

The heart is a vital part of reading the Bible. I have known people who have gone to seminaries to study the Bible and have left the seminary with their hearts further from God than when they arrived. This is not a statement about seminaries so much as a statement about our reasons for studying the Word of God.

Engaging our hearts challenges us to look at Scripture from more than an academic viewpoint. Many times we are so interested in the meaning of one word that we miss the plain meaning of the text. This is not an attempt to get rid of scholarship, but to recognize the role of our emotions and our will in the process of reading the Bible.

How do we do that? An example can be found in one of Jesus' most daunting teachings:

Then Jesus told his disciples, "If anyone would come after me, let him deny himself and take up his cross and follow me."

Matthew 16:24

If we focus our intellect upon this passage, we could do some research and discover that Jesus was approaching Jerusalem when He told this parable. As He came near the city, He wanted the imagery of the cross to become real to His disciples. He was prophetically foretelling the path ahead of them. His journey to Jerusalem was becoming a march to His death.

This analysis is fairly accurate, but if we stop there we lose something very important. When we add our own will to our reading, we ask, "What are the ramifications of this Scripture for me? Is there a command to be obeyed?" Then we realize that if we claim to be a follower of Jesus Christ, we are faced with an obvious question: "What am I supposed to deny?" What in my life needs to "die" in order for me to follow Jesus?

As we answer these questions, we may find a range of emotions welling up in our soul. We may be angry, or fearful, because it is becoming quite apparent what we need to give up in order to truly follow Jesus. Maybe it's some innocent comfort, or a relationship, or even a career path that needs to be reexamined. If we honestly engage this Scripture with our intellect, will, and emotions, we will face a crossroad that will either transform us in a full surrender to Jesus or create an even harder heart in us as we ignore what we are reading. This is more than just *reading the Bible*. This is an invitation to a change of heart.

You might be wondering how we can know the condition of our heart. The good news is God has given us the Scripture to expose, strengthen, and change the condition of our heart.

The Bible exposes the condition of our heart.

It's humbling to think that we don't judge the Bible, the Bible judges us. If we see the Bible in the way it speaks of itself—as the very Word of God—then our reaction to the Scriptures is more than just a reaction. It is a clue to the condition of our heart. Let's examine what Jesus said about this in Mark 4:

> Listen! A farmer went out to sow his seed. As he was scattering the seed, some fell along the path, and the birds came and ate it up. Some fell on rocky places, where it did not have much soil. It sprang up quickly, because the soil was shallow. But when the sun came up, the plants were scorched, and they withered because they had no root. Other seed fell among thorns, which grew up and choked the plants, so that they did not bear grain. Still other seed fell on good soil. It came up, grew and produced a crop, multiplying thirty, sixty, or even a hundred times. Then Jesus said, "He who has ears to hear, let him hear."
>
> Mark 4:3–9 NIV1984

One of the things that makes Jesus' teaching so remarkable is that He often set up barriers to His listeners. He wasn't interested in people simply hearing what He was saying; Jesus desired His followers to understand and obey what He said.

> When he was alone, the Twelve and the others around him asked him about the parables. He told them, "The secret of the kingdom of God has been given to you. But to those on the outside everything is said in parables so that, 'they may be ever seeing but never perceiving, and ever hearing but never understanding, otherwise they might turn and be forgiven!'" Then Jesus said to them, "Don't you understand this parable? How then will you understand any parable?"
>
> Mark 4:10–13 NIV 1984

In a sense, this is a gateway parable. According to Jesus, it is the key to understanding the other things He taught.

> The farmer sows the word. Some people are like seed along the path, where the word is sown. As soon as they hear it, Satan comes and takes away the word that was sown in them. Others, like seed sown on rocky places, hear the word and at once receive it with joy. But since they have no root, they last only a short time. When trouble or persecution comes because of the word, they quickly fall away. Still others, like seed sown among thorns, hear the word, but the worries of this life, the deceitfulness of wealth and the desires for other things come in and choke the word, making it unfruitful. Others, like seed sown on good soil, hear the word, accept it, and produce a crop—thirty, sixty or even a hundred times what was sown.
>
> Mark 4:14–20 NIV1984

Jesus' parable reveals the challenges that we all face concerning our heart. This parable tells us that we are in a war zone. There is an adversary who wants to steal the words of God from us; trouble and persecution will expose the tendency in all of us to use God for our own agendas. If we don't radically realign our lives according to the Scriptures, many distractions will block us from the benefits God has for us through His words. Then there are the people who experience a harvest. They will receive quite a reward if they just pay attention to the soil.

What do you think the soil is? We are all surrounded by adversity, trouble is unavoidable, and worries and temptations are in abundance. The difference is where our intellect, our emotions, and our will are focused. In other words, it takes the sowing of God's words into our lives to reveal the condition of our heart. Our job is to pay attention to the reactions (or lack of reactions) we experience. The wisdom of Proverbs speaks to us today:

> Keep vigilant watch over your heart,
> that's where life starts.
> Proverbs 4:23 THE MESSAGE

The Bible strengthens the condition of our heart.

When we are discouraged, the Scripture provides many ways to bring life back into our heart. The Psalms are filled with a wide range of emotions. Notice how David deals with his feelings of depression.

> Make me understand the way of thy precepts,
> and I will meditate on thy wondrous works.
> My soul melts away for sorrow,
> strengthen me according to thy word!
> Psalm 119:27–28 RSV

One of the traits of the Scriptures is that it can take a heart that is burdened with anxiety and give it peace. How many people have felt overwhelmed and then given those cares to God? Part of giving our cares over to God is actively reminding ourselves of God's promises. For some people, reading the Bible fits the bill in this regard; for others, hearing the Word spoken is more effective. Martin Luther, the great reformer of the church, wrote many times of preaching the gospel to himself. As Luther dealt with periods of depression and despair, he would go into a room and preach the Word until he felt his fears turn to faith in the Scriptures. Martin Luther regarded hearing the words of the Bible spoken aloud as vital to maintaining a heart toward God.

The Bible changes the condition of our heart.

There is so much more to say, but the last aspect of reading the Scriptures that we will address here is that the Scriptures can literally change the condition of our heart. This is more than strengthening, this is transformation. You may be reading this and saying, "I don't feel any of those things. I'm trying to read the Scriptures, and all I'm feeling is tired."

Don't be discouraged! Change is a process. We all start at different places, and the journey may be a long one, but as we begin this new path with God, the results will become evident over time.

If we think about Jesus' metaphor of seeds and harvest, we realize that we've probably been sowing a lot of other things into our lives. Our primary seed of choice may be anxiety, cynicism, or fear. These seeds produce their own harvest as well, but not a harvest that we want. For most of us, we have to learn to sow the seeds of Scripture into our lives at the same time that we are reaping the harvest of past thoughts and worldviews.

Genesis begins with the story of the Spirit of God hovering over the deep. Then God spoke, saying, "Let there be light." God has not stopped speaking, and, as beings created in His image,[5] God uses His spoken words to bring change within us. The apostle Paul writes about this in the book of Romans:

> But what does it say? "THE WORD IS NEAR YOU, IN YOUR MOUTH AND IN YOUR HEART"—that is, the word of faith which we are preaching, that if you confess with your mouth Jesus as Lord, and believe in your heart that God raised Him from the dead, you will be saved, for with the heart a person believes, resulting in righteousness, and with the mouth he confesses, resulting in salvation.
>
> Romans 10:8–10 NASB

What a mystery. To think that our confession of belief can cause such a revolution is both encouraging and challenging. Encouraging, in that it gives us hope that we can change, and challenging, in that change can be a scary uncertainty. The biblical pattern of change gives us the words that can transform our lives and help us to describe that life to others. We call that the gospel. Paul was not only demonstrating the word of faith, he was proclaiming it!

What causes this mystery to happen? That's what makes it a mystery. But the Bible speaks of itself not in dry, philosophical terms, but as a vibrant force. Look at what the writer of Hebrews tells us:

> For the word of God is living and powerful, and sharper than any two-edged sword, piercing even to the division of soul and spirit, and of joints and marrow, and is a discerner of the thoughts and intents of the heart. And there is no creature hidden from His sight, but all things are naked and open to the eyes of Him to whom we must give account.
>
> Hebrews 4:12–13 NKJV

It is no wonder that the two men on the road to Emmaus experienced a fresh passion as they heard Jesus speak to them. That fire wasn't from within them—it was from the very words of God being spoken! What happens when the words themselves have enough power to melt a cold heart, break a hard heart, or strengthen a weak heart? At that point, we have an intervention—God has broken through our world to speak to us. As New Testament scholar N. T. Wright wrote:

> Supposing Scripture, like the sacraments, is one of the points where heaven and earth overlap and interlock. Like all other such places, this is mysterious. It doesn't mean we can see at once what's going on. Indeed, it guarantees that we can't.[6]

Do we realize that when we open the Scriptures we are stepping into another realm? We are coming into a place where God can speak to us on a daily basis. Are we watching the condition of our heart as Scripture challenges us from another world? With the Holy Spirit and the Scriptures, God has provided all of His children with a way to know Him and in the process discover greater truths about ourselves.

Summary

If our mind, will, and emotions are not focused on knowing God, we could learn a lot about the Bible and yet not know Jesus. The good news is that the Bible itself can expose, strengthen, and change our heart as we read the Bible with faith. Therefore, to guard our heart through the reading of the Scriptures should be one of our most important duties of the day.

CHAPTER 3

Writing Styles in the Bible

The Bible belongs to literature, that is, it is a piece of art.

Clyde S. Kilby

In 2010, twenty-seven hundred marine biologists consolidated their research into the Census of Marine Life.[1] Ten years in the making, this work categorizes the latest discoveries in ocean species. The number of recent findings is staggering. From the discovery of a giant squid to "Jurassic shrimp" that were supposed to have been extinct since the days of the dinosaurs, researchers involved with this project, over the last year alone, cataloged twelve hundred new species with five thousand more awaiting a formal description, bringing the total number of known marine animals to over two hundred and fifty thousand.

The scientists who worked closely on the project have expressed a sense of constant wonder. As one of the vice chairs of the project said, "Life astonished us everywhere we looked. The discoveries of new species and habitats both advanced science and inspired artists with their extraordinary beauty."[2]

If God displays that much diversity and creativity in His universe, then it should not surprise us to find that the Bible is written in many different styles in order to reveal all the aspects of His character and deeds.

As we saw in the introduction, forty-four authors from many locations in the ancient world wrote the Bible. When we look at the sixty-six books the Bible contains, we find many different genres of literature. It seems that God delights not only in using written words but also to present those words in different formats.

For example, when we read 1 and 2 Samuel in the Old Testament, we see a historical narrative of Israel. These books stick to the facts—there are names and places, dates and events. It's important to read them as the authors intended—as accounts that tell us the story of God's faithfulness to the promises He made to the Jewish people.

An honest reading of these accounts would see dysfunctional uses of power and sexuality, betrayals of trust, and much more. It is far from a clean, happy world, and, if we are honest, we would see many parallels to the behavior of people today. It seems that even though civilization has progressed, the heart of man has remained the same.

A common mistake is to think that the Bible condones the events that it records. This would be like blaming newspapers for the terrible events they write about. The historical accounts of the Old Testament describe a broken world, but the Old Testament also points to a God who is faithful in the midst of a rebellious people. The star of the Old Testament narratives is not David or Ruth. The true star of these accounts is God, who throughout promises the coming of the One who will be the ultimate king not only of Israel, but of the entire earth.

The New Testament Gospels also deal with dates and places. Look at what Luke wrote at the beginning of his account of the life of Jesus:

Inasmuch as many have undertaken to compile a narrative of the things that have been accomplished among us, just as those who from the beginning were eyewitnesses and ministers of the word have delivered them to us, it seemed good to me also, having followed all things closely for some time past, to write an orderly account for you, most excellent Theophilus, that you may have certainty concerning the things you have been taught.

Luke 1:1–4

Luke also wrote the Acts of the Apostles (the book of Acts), which records the adventures of the first followers of Jesus. The book of Acts gives us insight into life in the early church as the Holy Spirit was poured out upon Jewish and non-Jewish believers. A Bible atlas is helpful when we read the book of Acts, because it moves quickly from Jerusalem to Europe as churches were being established throughout the Roman world.

The Epistles are letters that were written to many of the churches that were founded and mentioned in the book of Acts. They are filled with theological discussion, as these churches were dealing with all sorts of problems. We'll examine the Epistles further in chapter 5.

In contrast to the books of historical narrative or the theology of the Epistles, we can't approach the Psalms in the same way. Most of the Psalms were songs meant to be sung in the Jewish temple for worship. When we look at the Psalms, it is important to realize that they were predominantly created to express emotional prayers to God. They are beautiful poems that can't be looked at in the same way that we examine the writings of the apostle Paul in the New Testament. They are not a literal record of events or an explanation of theology.

We will examine the poetry of the Bible in chapter 7, but it's important to understand these differences from the very beginning. Otherwise, we can misunderstand and even misuse the Psalms for inaccurate doctrinal stances instead of seeing them as guides for how to express ourselves to God and understand His ways. We can miss the intent of the ancient authors and, more important, the original Author who inspired them to write these powerful songs.

This in no way takes away the power of the Psalms as God's words. In His good pleasure, God used a unique form of expression to help us understand both Him and ourselves. In a sense, facts are not enough to describe this God. His nature is so beyond us that it takes a number of different ways to exalt Him.

Another literary tool found throughout the Bible is metaphor. A metaphor uses a word or phrase not literally, but to create an image that is used as a way to compare things. For example, Jesus uses metaphor when He states:

> I am the good shepherd, the good shepherd lays down His life for the sheep.
>
> John 10:11 NASB

Jesus uses shepherding to describe himself and sheep to describe His followers. (This sounds romantic until you understand the nature of sheep!) This metaphor also parallels Psalm 23, where David calls the Lord his shepherd. In using this metaphor, Jesus achieves a number of things: He establishes a picture of tender care and selfless sacrifice for His followers, and He gives them a glimpse of His true identity.

You can even find humor in the Bible, including sarcasm. As the Israelites are being led out of Egypt toward the Promised

Land, notice the contrast between verses two and three in Deuteronomy, chapter 1 (NLT):

> Normally it takes only eleven days to travel from Mount Sinai to Kadesh-barnea, going by way of Mount Seir.

> But forty years after the Israelites left Egypt . . .

Deuteronomy is the last of five books that describe the Jewish journey out of slavery. These two verses are a jab at how long the journey was supposed to last, and how long it actually took!

In another passage, we get some insight into the internal challenges the early church faced with this account of the dramatic conversion of Saul of Tarsus into the apostle Paul:

> When [Saul] came to Jerusalem, he was trying to associate with the disciples, but they were all afraid of him, not believing that he was a disciple. But Barnabas took hold of him and brought him to the apostles and described to them how he had seen the Lord on the road, and that He had talked to him, and how at Damascus [Saul] had spoken out boldly in the name of Jesus. And he was with them, moving about freely in Jerusalem, speaking out boldly in the name of the Lord. And he was talking and arguing with the Hellenistic Jews, but they were attempting to put him to death. But when the brethren learned of it, they brought him down to Caesarea and sent him away to Tarsus.
>
> So the church throughout all Judea and Galilee and Samaria enjoyed peace, being built up, and going on in the fear of the Lord and in the comfort of the Holy Spirit, it continued to increase.
>
> Acts 9:26–31 NASB

At first, the leaders at Jerusalem were amazed when they realized that the Jewish bounty hunter, Saul, had become a follower of Jesus. But the very drive that made Saul a successful persecutor of Christians now made him a source of irritation to everyone around him in Jerusalem. It became so tense that the brothers sent Saul back to his hometown!

Then notice Luke's subtle commentary: After Saul was gone, they experienced peace. It's almost as if the church in Jerusalem breathed a sigh of relief at the departure of such an energetic (and explosive) personality.

The Bible also portrays dramatic tension. Take this passage in Genesis:

> After these things God tested Abraham and said to him, "Abraham!" And he said, "Here I am." He said, "Take your son, your only son Isaac, whom you love, and go to the land of Moriah, and offer him there as a burnt offering on one of the mountains of which I shall tell you."
>
> Genesis 22:1–2

The story unfolds as Abraham takes his only son up the mountain, binds him, and then lifts a knife in order to offer him as a sacrifice to God:

> Then Abraham reached out his hand and took the knife to slaughter his son. But the angel of the LORD called to him from heaven and said, "Abraham, Abraham!" And he said, "Here I am." He said, "Do not lay your hand on the boy or do anything to him, for now I know that you fear God, seeing you have not withheld your son, your only son, from me."
>
> Genesis 22:10–12

There are many other places where the Bible uses drama. We can feel the frustration and anguish in the prophet Jeremiah's young soul over a nation that has turned its back on God. This is a very challenging calling for a young man, and by the time we get to chapter 20, Jeremiah snaps at God:

O LORD, You have deceived me and I was deceived;
You have overcome me and prevailed.
I have become a laughingstock all day long,
Everyone mocks me.
For each time I speak, I cry aloud,
I proclaim violence and destruction,
Because for me the word of the LORD has resulted
In reproach and derision all day long.

Jeremiah 20:7–8 NASB

Jeremiah hates his job, yet he can't keep silent. He is a man who is gripped by God, yet as far as things on this earth go, his future is not very bright.

These are just a few examples of the various styles the Bible uses to communicate God's nature to mankind. One could say that because there are so many kinds of people, it takes a lot of different expressions to connect with them. The psalmist sings of how excellent is the name of the Lord in all the earth.[3] Just as nature is God's general revelation, Scripture is God's special revelation. Many times the wonder of this marvelous world leads us to the wonder of God's words.

Scientist Francis Collins headed the Human Genome project when they mapped our genetic code and released it for the world to see. What many people don't know is that Collins is a Christian. He recounts his encounter with Christ during a hiking trip:

On a beautiful fall day, as I was hiking in the Cascade Mountains during my first trip west of the Mississippi, the majesty and beauty of God's creation overwhelmed my resistance. As I rounded a corner and saw a beautiful and unexpected frozen waterfall, hundreds of feet high, I knew the search was over. The next morning, I knelt in the dewy grass as the sun rose and surrendered to Jesus Christ.[4]

As we look at the diverse expressions of Scripture in the following chapters, I pray that your understanding of God will be expanded. May you find the same beauty of God's creation in His written words.

Summary

When God decided to reveal himself to His children in Scripture, He used the same creativity and ingenuity that we see in nature. The different styles of literature that God uses are uniquely crafted to reach people in a variety of ways. This creativity challenges us to expand our horizons when we think about God and also empowers us to be creative in how we live before Him.

CHAPTER 4

Abraham: Friend of God

Much of this book is written to help you make sense of the Bible, and in so doing, we need to acknowledge that the Bible is an epic story about God and how He interacts with His creation. The categories this book presents are helpful tools to explain the Scriptures, but in order to fully understand the Bible, we also need to look at individual stories of the Bible and how they connect.

Therefore, we are going to briefly explore four major figures in the Bible. There are many more, but I have chosen Abraham, Moses, David, and Jesus in the hope that their narratives will help you better understand the big picture of the story told in the Bible, and in so doing, give you some insights into how God could be bringing your story into His story. Each narrative is not intended to cover all of the details of these men's lives, but to give you a simple overview. So in that spirit, we will start with Abraham, who is considered the father of our faith. It may surprise you to know that Abraham came from a culture and religious tradition that was totally at odds with God's character.

Abram's Family

We can only speculate how Abram felt when God first spoke to him in Genesis 12. He was the son of Terah, a Chaldean (Chaldea was located in what is currently southern Iraq), who moved to Canaan (in what is now Turkey). The Bible tells us that Terah was a man who worshiped other gods,[1] so Abram was probably raised around ceremonies to the gods of that time, such as Mot, a god of death, and Molech, who required child sacrifice. This important point will help us understand Abraham better as we look at his life.

What prompted Terah to leave the city of Ur, a cultured city in the land of the Chaldeans, for the warlord-dominated world of Canaan? It's hard to say, but the Bible notes that Terah's youngest son, Haran, died at Ur in the prime of his life. The death of a child was surely as devastating then as it is today, and since Scripture mentions Haran's death as an important fact, we would not be reaching too far to see Terah as a grief-stricken father looking for a new home that wouldn't remind him of his loss.

But Haran had a son before he died. Young Lot was now in the care of the household of Terah, and we can see how Abram, the oldest son in this family and childless at this point, would bond with Lot in a unique way. This bond would play a major role later on in their lives.

God Calls Abram

In ancient cultures, the oldest son was expected to carry on the family name and business. He was the one who received the family inheritance. This tradition created a crisis for Abram in Genesis 12, because in this context God's first words to Abram were very difficult:

> Leave your country, your family, and your father's home for a land that I will show you. I'll make you a great nation and bless you. I'll make you famous, you'll be a blessing. I'll bless those who bless you, those who curse you I'll curse. All the families of the Earth will be blessed through you.
>
> 12:1–3 THE MESSAGE

Remember that at this point, there was no Old Testament or New Testament—there was only a voice. Hearing the voice of a god was disturbing enough, but the implications of what this god said would be life-changing.

Abram would have to give up his father's inheritance in order to obey this directive. Everything would go to Abram's younger brother, Nahor, and Abram would lose his social standing in his father's household. Abram would be seen as a deserter of his family. On top of that, God didn't tell Abram where he was going—He only commanded Abram to venture into the wilderness.

The wilderness was synonymous with danger and even death. There were no hotels or restaurants along the way! The land was filled with wild beasts and bands of thieves, and Abram could have come upon an unknown king with an army who could kill him. The warlords of Canaan offered protection from the realities of the wilderness. Abram would be leaving all of that protection behind.

In other words, God's first words to Abram cut against all his sensibilities.

Sometimes people think it was easier for the people in the Bible to believe God, but that isn't what we see in the Bible. If the Bible is God's chief communication with us, then there is honesty in the text that gives us permission to wrestle with Him. As we will see, it was not Abram's moral character that qualified him to become the father of our faith. On the contrary, the New Testament writer Paul reflects upon Abraham centuries later when he writes:

> Abraham was, humanly speaking, the founder of our Jewish nation. What did he discover about being made right with God? If his good deeds had made him acceptable to God, he would have had something to boast about. But that was not God's way. For the Scriptures tell us, "Abraham believed God, and God counted him as righteous because of his faith."
>
> Romans 4:1–3 NLT

Abram looked at the promises of God's blessing; then he looked at the dangers of the wilderness, and Abram believed that God's words were greater than his surroundings. God would sustain him in the midst of the wilderness. It was belief, not ability, that uniquely positioned Abram in the story of God, and it was God, not Abram, who cultivated this relationship through further visitations.

Abram's Character Flaws

You would think that Abram would be above all of the struggles we face due to his unique relationship with God, but that was not the case. We begin to see some of Abram's character flaws when hardship hits his life:

> Now there was a famine in the land, and Abram went down to Egypt to live there for a while because the famine was severe. As he was about to enter Egypt, he said to his wife, Sarai, "I know what a beautiful woman you are. When the Egyptians see

you, they will say, 'This is his wife.' Then they will kill me but will let you live. Say you are my sister, so that I will be treated well for your sake and my life will be spared because of you."

Genesis 12:10–13 NIV1984

This pattern repeats itself in Genesis 20 with the king of Gerar. What makes these accounts even more profound is that God promised to bless the offspring of Abram, so when Abram quickly gave his wife over to other kings to spare his life, he was also giving up the source and future of his blessing.

God protected Sarai from any romantic advances from these kings, and once again shows us that God's mercy is greater than Abram's (or our) weaknesses. In an eerie foreshadowing of later events, God sent plagues upon Egypt, and Pharaoh discovered that his dilemma was linked to his new bride:

> So Pharaoh called Abram and said, "What is this you have done to me? Why did you not tell me that she was your wife? Why did you say, 'She is my sister,' so that I took her for my wife? Now then, here is your wife, take her, and go." And Pharaoh gave men orders concerning him, and they sent him away with his wife and all that he had.

Genesis 12:18–20

God was more than capable of upholding His purposes, even when Abram was ready to give those purposes up in the interest of his own safety. The stories of Abram's lying (or half-lies, since Sarai *was* his half-sister) help us to determine the true hero of these stories. It is not Abram or Sarai—it is God, whose faithfulness to imperfect people would culminate thousands of years later at the cross of Calvary, when Jesus Christ would cover over our sins in the same way that God covered over Abram's

49

sins, by getting us to believe what He says instead of what we see in front of us.

Abram, Lot, and Melchizedek

Meanwhile, Abram's nephew Lot was ready to venture out on his own in Genesis 13. It would not be presumptuous to assume that Abram took on the role of a father to Lot when Haran passed away, but now Lot wanted to see what he could do without help from his uncle Abram.

We are not sure if Abram had shared with Lot what God had spoken to him, but after the Egyptian incident, it should have been apparent that Abram possessed unique favor with God. That didn't seem to matter to Lot, however, because the beauty of the valley of Sodom and Gomorrah overshadowed everything else that Lot could see.

This story would not end well for Lot, but he was determined to get out from under Abram's shadow, and in doing so Lot also came out from under God's blessing. As soon as Lot moved into the lush valley next to Sodom, he was taken as a prisoner by foreign kings simply because he was in the wrong place at the wrong time.

By this point, Abram had enough men working for him that he could gather a small army and rescue Lot from his captors. The rescue was so impressive that a new king who had not been mentioned before appeared—Melchizedek of Salem. Salem was an area that included the city later called Jerusalem,[2] and it is in this account that Abram is called a Hebrew for the first time, so in a sense this story brings greater definition to both the land and the people who will later be set apart by God for His purposes.

Melchizedek also brought more definition of who this God is. In using the term *Most High God,* Melchizedek gave Abram new insight that this was not just one god of many who favored Abram; this was the one true God.

The New Testament writer of Hebrews describes the unique figure of Melchizedek this way:

> For this Melchizedek, king of Salem, priest of the Most High God, who met Abraham as he was returning from the slaughter of the kings and blessed him, to whom also Abraham apportioned a tenth part of all the spoils, was first of all, by the translation of his name, king of righteousness, and then also king of Salem, which is king of peace. Without father, without mother, without genealogy, having neither beginning of days nor end of life, but made like the Son of God, he remains a priest perpetually.
>
> Hebrews 7:1–3 NASB

This mysterious king of peace, who was also a priest, was yet another foreshadowing of a future king/priest who mysteriously comes to the earth to reveal who God really is. But that is for a later story.

God's Promise to Abram

Abram upheld his allegiance to the God who met him repeatedly, but he had some concerns. He still did not have a son, so he asked God if he could give his inheritance to a trusted member of Abram's household, but God was adamant:

> Then the word of the LORD came to him: "This man will not be your heir, but a son coming from your own body will be your heir." He took him outside and said, "Look up at the heavens and count the stars—if indeed you can count them." Then he said to him, "So shall your offspring be."
>
> Abram believed the LORD, and he credited it to him as righteousness.
>
> Genesis 15:4–6 NIV

Abram's belief was finalized in a grisly ceremony in which animals were cut in half and each party walked between the sides of the animals. This action said, "May the same be done to me if I break this agreement." But Abram's ceremony had a dramatic twist—only God walked between the animals; Abram was not required to do so. This would have spoken volumes to an ancient reader, for this put the entire burden upon God and not Abram to uphold their agreement. It seemed that only God could fulfill the agreement, or covenant, and God was willing to put His own life on the line to see Abram's descendants become as numerous as the stars. We will see later that God did fulfill His promise to Abram, though it required His death on the cross.

Ishmael

It seems that, by this point, Abram should have been clear as to how God would provide an heir, but this was not the case. Sarai became impatient, so she urged Abram to have a child with her maidservant, Hagar. Since a son was necessary to preserve the family line, this was an acceptable practice in ancient times, but just because things are acceptable doesn't mean they are right. Things didn't go well for Hagar when she had her son, Ishmael. Abram loved Ishmael, and was grooming him to be the heir of the family, but Sarai's jealousy eventually caused Hagar and Ishmael to be cast out of the clan into the wilderness, and Abram's heart broke as he watched his sixteen-year-old son leave him.

Isaac

Even in the midst of this failure, God appeared again to Abram to give him a sign of their covenant: circumcision. God also changed Abram's name to Abraham, meaning "father of a multitude," and Sarai to Sarah, which means "princess," and told them again that they would become pregnant with a child.

The absurdity of these names and God's promise was not lost on Abraham and Sarah. Sarah actually laughed about it, and in a satirical twist, when God proved to be true and gave them a son, they named him Isaac, or "laughter," because Sarah's cynical laughter turned into the laughter of joy. The name of her child became a reminder of how God's patience and loving-kindness can heal the deepest pain in our hearts.

The Sacrifice of Isaac

One of the best-known stories of Abraham is also the most controversial: the offering of Isaac as a sacrifice on Mount Moriah.

> Some time later God tested Abraham. He said to him, "Abraham!"

> "Here I am," he replied. Then God said, "Take your son, your only son, Isaac, whom you love, and go to the region of Moriah. Sacrifice him there as a burnt offering on one of the mountains I will tell you about."

> Genesis 22:1–2 NIV

The horror of God asking for a human sacrifice gives many people second thoughts about what kind of God this is. But let's look at this story from a perspective we may not have had before.

Human sacrifice was a common practice in those days. There are many ancient documents that tell us that sacrificing children was seen as a way to promote fertility in the land, so when God told Abraham to sacrifice his son, Isaac, though very difficult, it was not a new concept to him. It would have made sense to him that if God were going to bless Abraham in this way, a sacrifice of some kind would be necessary.

But this is where the story becomes radical. As Abraham had Isaac bound on the altar, with a raised knife that was about to plunge into Isaac's heart, God told Abraham to stop. To the ancient mindset, stopping the sacrifice would anger the gods and bring a curse upon the land. Our current culture is shocked that God tells Abraham to sacrifice his son, but the reader of that day would have been shocked that God told Abraham to stop.

What if God was using the religious traditions of Abraham's day to adjust his view of God? Could setting up the sacrifice, then stopping it, not only be a test of Abraham's willingness to obey but also a proclamation to the ancient world that this God is like no other? This is speculation, but the ancient mindset was that man needed to bring the sacrifice to appease the gods—but the God of Abraham would not allow it; God himself would provide the sacrifice. A ram that suddenly appeared in a thicket nearby would not only become the sacrifice, it would become an eternal reminder that God is our provider. He knows the things that we assume about life and the world around us and provides insight; He meets us in our deep flaws and brings healing; He sees us in our sin and provides a way out.

We should gain great hope from the way God worked with Abraham, because we too have many cultural assumptions about God and the world around us that may not be accurate. If God could use Abraham with all of his flaws and misunderstand-ings, we can be assured that He can use us as well. Abraham is a witness of God's faithfulness to His promises as all of us stumble toward redemption.

CHAPTER 5

The Gospels

The gospel, to me, is simply irresistible.

Blaise Pascal, philosopher
and mathematician

The film *Vantage Point* brought an interesting storytelling approach to movie fans. The film portrayed a fictional attempt to assassinate the president of the United States during a diplomatic trip to Spain. But what made the film unique was that it kept retelling each segment of the story from the viewpoint of a different character.

First, we see the series of events from the perspective of a television producer assigned to film the trip. Then we see the same series of events from the view of Secret Service agents who were protecting the president, then from the vantage point of a Spanish police officer, and a final perspective from an American tourist. Each pass on the series of events gives us a fuller picture of what happened that day.

This is a good way to understand the Gospels. Each of the four gospels is a firsthand account of what Jesus said and did. Matthew helps us understand the account of Mark better, and Luke uses exact language to help us with the details. Meanwhile, John records events that none of the other three even mention. As you learn how to read the Bible, the Gospels are a great place to begin.

Like the movie, each gospel helps us grasp what was going on during the life of Jesus by providing us with a unique viewpoint. There is no real information about why there are four. According to scholars Gordon Fee and Douglas Stuart, one reason could be that different communities needed different accounts. It is interesting that there is no gospel directly attributed to Jesus. As Fee and Stuart have written, "They are not books *by* Jesus but *about* Jesus."[1]

If we understand this, we are able to see that the authors of the Gospels never intended that we read their writings as modern biographies but as memoirs. A modern biography is more concerned with the sequence of events, while a memoir has a greater emphasis on the themes that emerged from that life.

An important thing to remember is that the apostles lived before the Enlightenment, which changed the way people interpreted information. As products of the Enlightenment, we want to break information down into sections that fit neatly together. This may be hard for us to understand, but the gospel writers were not that concerned about all of the events lining up and matching with each other. Instead, they were more focused on writing from their own individual perspective about what Jesus did and said.

This can ease a lot of confusion when we read variations of the same account in different gospels. People who talk about the seeming contradictions in the gospel accounts are trying to treat the Gospels like a textbook. But each author grouped his recollections of Jesus differently for his unique reading audience as he was writing under the inspiration of the Holy Spirit. This does not take away from the power and clarity of the Scriptures at all. If anything, knowing this should help us to more fully understand what God was saying through each particular author.

With this approach, the historical setting of each gospel plays an important part in understanding what God was saying (and is saying) to His people.

Matthew focused on a Jewish reader. That's why he starts his gospel with a genealogy. To trace the lineage of Jesus back to David would be a big deal to a Hebrew who was wondering if Jesus was the Jewish Messiah. Matthew also refers to the Old Testament quite a bit to back up his accounts of Jesus' life and teachings.

Mark wrote more for the Romans, who couldn't care less about Hebrew genealogy. Mark's gospel is filled with action. By the fourteenth verse of chapter 1, Mark already records Jesus preaching about the kingdom of God. Mark loses little time, and his gospel is regarded as the fast-paced account.

Luke was a Gentile (non-Jewish) physician who wrote for sophisticated non-Jewish readers. He records in great detail in order that Gentile readers would understand the universal appeal of the gospel. Luke also wrote the book of Acts.

John's gospel is reflective and geared for the Greek reader. The famous first line, "In the beginning was the Word . . ." sets the stage for an account that not only reveals that Jesus is the Son of God but also refutes the pagan mystery religions that were beginning to flourish around him. John exhorts his readers from the beginning that Jesus is the lens through which to see all of creation, and he ends his gospel by saying that even creation could not contain all of the things that Jesus did.

It is important to note that the apostles did not simply write whatever they wanted to. They were constrained to write about what actually happened. In that sense, the Gospels are history books. They are filled with names and places and they reference historical figures that are found in other ancient writings. (For example: Jesus Christ is recognized in many other ancient texts outside of the Bible.[2])

The amount of detail the Gospels hold tells us that these accounts were not written as myths, but were expected to be read as actual accounts of what Jesus said and did. Jesus did use parables and other allegorical teaching strategies, but the Gospels were not written as symbols of something else.

C. S. Lewis was the author of the bestselling children's book *The Lion, the Witch, and the Wardrobe*. What many people don't know is that he was also regarded as a world expert in medieval literature. He taught at Cambridge and Oxford and wrote a number of critical works that are still used in universities today. When Lewis began to read the Gospels, he made this observation:

> I have been reading poems, romances, vision literature, legends, and myths all my life. I know what they are like. I know none of them are like this. Of this [gospel] text there are only two possible views. Either this is reportage . . . or else, some unknown writer in the second century, without known predecessors or successors, suddenly anticipated the whole technique of modern novelistic, realistic narrative.[3]

In other words, the Gospels were written in such a way that you can't approach them as fanciful accounts about Jesus, but only for what they are—the chronicling of eyewitness accounts.

In these accounts, Jesus proclaims the kingdom of heaven everywhere He goes. He wants people to understand that God is doing something new, and therefore, He uses many different teaching styles to get His points across.

It seems that the kingdom of heaven is hard for us to grasp in a straightforward way, so Jesus used stories, or parables, to explain how the kingdom of heaven works. This was so important to Jesus that most of His teachings are in the form of parables. Since parables are emphasized so much in the life of Jesus, we would do well to understand them.

Parables are stories that function as a lens that allows us to both see truth and correct distortions. Because they are stories, they can have a powerful impact upon our thinking and imagination. But parables can also cause some misunderstandings because they assume you know the reference points of the story. Knowing to whom Jesus was speaking makes all the difference in reading the parables. Let me give you a famous example.

When we read about the Prodigal Son in Luke 15, we are deeply moved by the story of the younger brother who squandered his inheritance:

> But when he came to himself, he said, "How many of my father's hired servants have bread enough and to spare, and I perish with hunger! I will arise and go to my father, and will say to him, 'Father, I have sinned against heaven and before you, and I am no longer worthy to be called your son. Make me like one of your hired servants.'"
>
> And he arose and came to his father. But when he was still a great way off, his father saw him and had compassion, and ran and fell on his neck and kissed him. And the son said to him, "Father, I have sinned against heaven and in your sight, and am no longer worthy to be called your son."

But the father said to his servants, "Bring out the best robe and put it on him, and put a ring on his hand and sandals on his feet. And bring the fatted calf here and kill it, and let us eat and be merry, for this my son was dead and is alive again, he was lost and is found." And they began to be merry.

Luke 15:17–24 NKJV

But if we don't recognize that Jesus was telling this parable to religious leaders, we can totally miss that Jesus was equating his listeners with an elder brother in the story—a son who was just as distant from his father as his younger immoral sibling. As one pastor states, this is not the story of the Prodigal Son, but of Two Sons. Both were trying to manipulate their Father—the younger through rebellion and the older through obedience![4]

Jesus used other teaching styles as well. Look at this statement in Matthew:

And if your right hand causes you to sin, cut it off and throw it away. For it is better that you lose one of your members than that your whole body go into hell.

Matthew 9:43

This is not an injunction to cut off your hand. (If we took this entire passage literally, there would be a lot of one-eyed, one-footed, and one-handed Christians!) Jesus was using hyperbole, or an exaggerated statement, to make a strong point about how serious the ultimate judgment of hell is. Our view of the eternal determines how we live today. In other words, just because we don't see hell doesn't make it less of a reality. This teaching style was common then and still is today. Once again, this does not take away the role this teaching has as God's Word. It helps us understand it better.

Finally, there is something that we should remember when we approach the gospel accounts of Jesus' life.

There are many forms of idolatry in today's world but none so blatant as America's idolatry of celebrities. The pattern usually plays out like this: Someone who has talent and ambition works hard and rises to fame. Once they have achieved success, celebrities become hard to get to, and a glamorous persona is created. Photographers follow their every move. Magazines chronicle their antics. Then someone writes the "kiss-and-tell" book that lets us know the "behind the scenes" issues that only the inner circle of friends and acquaintances would see. Most of the time the exposé is not very flattering, and we can't even be sure it is all true.

In a way, that is what happened to Jesus. When His ministry started, crowds of people followed Him. The Gospels tell us that Jesus would avoid cities because the attention was affecting His ability to move about freely. But the implication of Jesus' teaching was undeniable—He was claiming to be God. This caused a lot of turmoil all over Judea. Jesus became so controversial that they crucified Him in an attempt to squelch the movement of the followers He was amassing.

You would think that after Jesus was killed, those closest to Him would let people know all the embarrassing stuff no one saw or heard but Him. But when Jesus' inner circle wrote about His life, their "kiss-and-tell" books became the Gospels. Those who were closest to Him validated His claims!

This should help us to realize that the authors of the Gospels had no vested interest in writing these accounts. There was no apparent personal benefit for their efforts. They wrote the Gospels because the events *happened*. As we will see in the apostle Paul's writings, these accounts were written by men who were impacted by something so profound, so real, that they were willing to lay everything on the line to get these accounts in writing. In fact, many of them were killed for doing so.

The four gospel accounts of Jesus Christ provide us with a complex and riveting portrait of a man who claimed to be God. These records of His life, death, and resurrection literally changed the world then and are still changing it today. As these accounts proclaim that the kingdom of God is here, they invite us to join God in His epic story of renewing the earth through Jesus Christ.

We have an opportunity to respond to that invitation. Join God in His story. When you do, your story gains new meaning and purpose in ways that you could never imagine.

Summary

Each writer of the Gospels wrote a unique account of Jesus for a particular audience. As we read the gospel accounts, we see Jesus using various teaching styles to make His points fully understood. The life and message of Jesus are not only the center of the Christian faith, they are meant to be the center of our lives as well. The Gospels call us to follow Jesus with all our heart, mind, soul, and strength.

CHAPTER 6

The Epistles

Paul expressed what the apostles all discovered: that this retelling
of the ancient story, climaxing now in Jesus, carried power—power
to change minds, hearts, and lives.

N. T. Wright, New Testament scholar

Have you ever had the opportunity to read letters or emails
that were written to someone else? Maybe you found
letters that your parents wrote to each other during their engagement. Or maybe a friend forwarded you a number of email
exchanges that he or she was having with someone else. When we
get a peek into these personal documents, we are exposed to in-
timate information that can be both enlightening and confusing.

Many times they refer to prior events. A line might read,
"What a time we had over the holidays! I'll be laughing about
the cake for weeks!" You may feel privileged (or uncomfortable)
accessing this dialogue, but unless you know what happened

with the cake, it will be hard to grasp what the writer meant by her comment.

Understanding this helps us as we approach the Epistles, which are the letters included in the New Testament. The Epistles have provided the framework for important beliefs, like how Jesus makes us righteous, the work of the Holy Spirit in our lives, and the role of the church. These letters have given the people of God some of the most practical applications for what it means to be a follower of Jesus Christ.

The apostle Paul is attributed with the largest group of letters, but many letters in the New Testament are associated with the apostles John, Peter, James, and a short one by Jude. Each epistle was written in response to a particular set of circumstances. In order to understand what they mean, you must have some knowledge of the situations the letters were addressing in the first place.

You may be wondering why letters became a part of the New Testament. These documents were written specifically to instruct churches. Notice what Paul writes to the church in Colossae:

> And when this epistle is read among you, cause that it be read also in the church of the Laodiceans; and that ye likewise read the epistle from Laodicea.
>
> Colossians 4:16 KJV

Paul intended that his letter to the Colossians be read aloud to the entire community. He also references a letter to Laodicea, which hasn't yet been found. These letters were written with the goal of setting things straight or bringing right thinking and right living to these communities, thereby helping them align themselves with the gospel. The Epistles are doctrinally rich and provide insights that are essential to Christians.

The writers of the Epistles wanted to make sure that the spiritual deposit they received as eyewitnesses of Christ would be properly handed on to the next generation. On the eve of his death, Peter wrote:

> Therefore, I will always be ready to remind you of these things, even though you already know them, and have been established in the truth which is present with you. I consider it right, as long as I am in this earthly dwelling, to stir you up by way of reminder, knowing that the laying aside of my earthly dwelling is imminent, as also our Lord Jesus Christ has made clear to me. And I will also be diligent that at any time after my departure you will be able to call these things to mind.
>
> 2 Peter 1:12–15 NASB

From the early church on, these letters have been seen as authoritative, given by the Holy Spirit for the church to obey and to teach others.[1] So with this in mind, let's examine how to get the most out of the Epistles.

The first thing we have to consider is the context in which they were written. What circumstances were they addressing? This is where some knowledge of ancient history is important.

A Bible dictionary and a study Bible are great tools to use as you discover the background of each epistle. (See appendix B.) You will find, for example, that the epistle to the Galatians was a response to Hebrew teachers telling Gentile Christians they needed to live according to the Jewish laws. Look at this entry from the *New Bible Dictionary*:

> The "churches of Galatia" had evidently been visited by Judaizers who cast doubt on Paul's apostolic status and insisted that, in addition to the faith in Christ, it was necessary to be circumcised and to conform in other respects to the Jewish law in order to attain salvation.[2]

In a sense, the freedom of the gospel was about to be re-framed by people who believed that Christians needed to keep all the law of Moses. This would have seriously hindered the work of God among non-Jewish communities, so it should be no wonder that Paul starts this letter with a passion and an urgency that is jarring:

> I am astonished that you are so quickly deserting him who called you in the grace of Christ and turning to a different gospel—not that there is another gospel, but there are some who trouble you and want to pervert the gospel of Christ. But even if we, or an angel from heaven, should preach to you a gospel contrary to that which we preached to you, let him be accursed.
>
> Galatians 1:6–8 RSV

Paul wanted to make clear that even though Christianity came from Jewish roots, the gospel comes through grace alone. To add any other deeds of righteousness to the work of Christ would pervert the gospel—it would no longer be the good news of God through Jesus Christ.

The next thing we have to consider in understanding the Epistles is that our generation has many biases, or filters, that shape the way we view the world around us. These filters may cloud our understanding of a text from a different era. Staying with Ephesians, Paul addresses slavery in a passage that has been commonly misapplied:

> Slaves, obey your earthly masters with respect and fear, and with sincerity of heart, just as you would obey Christ. Obey them not only to win their favor when their eye is on you, but like slaves of Christ, doing the will of God from your heart. Serve wholeheartedly, as if you were serving the Lord, not men, because

you know that the Lord will reward everyone for whatever good he does, whether he is slave or free.

Ephesians 6:5–8 NIV1984

Many people see this passage as an endorsement of slavery. But there are some cultural filters that we need to deal with first:

- Slavery in that time was not like the form of slavery that existed in America before the Civil War. Even though slavery was not easy, slaves had rights. They rarely worked as slaves all of their lives, and they were usually paid for their services. Many times slaves were better off than the free men in their area, because slaves had better pay and living situations.

- Slavery was an accepted institution of the ancient world when these letters were written. To have slaves in that day was not regarded as unusual or wrong.

When Paul wrote this, he was addressing the harsh realities of his culture, but he didn't stop there. Notice the very next verse:

And masters, treat your slaves in the same way. Do not threaten them, since you know that he who is both their Master and yours is in heaven, and there is no favoritism with him.

Ephesians 6:9 NIV1984

Paul went where few ancient writers would dare to go—he placed the slave owner on equal status with the slave. When you look at other places in the New Testament where Paul writes about slavery,[3] it becomes obvious that Paul sees slavery as an institution that needs to bow to the new realities of the gospel.

Paul was sowing the seeds of future change into a practice that was accepted worldwide.

As we have examined the Epistles, we first looked at the ancient context to help us understand what the letter meant to the original reader. Then we acknowledged that our modern bias has created filters that affect how we interpret Scripture. Now we are ready to apply the text to our current situation. We have talked about some of the differences we encounter between the ancient world and our world today. It is time to address the things that are constant through the ages: God and humankind.

When we look at the Bible from the beginning to the end, we see a common pattern: God is consistent while people are inconsistent. God gives commands and makes promises, and His people consistently disobey those commands. As a result, they fall apart spiritually. The Epistles reinforce this story in an amazing fashion. Here is a short summary of each of the Epistles.

Romans—The most systematic of Paul's epistles. This letter explains the plan of salvation for the Gentiles and the Jews.

1 Corinthians—The Corinthian church was plagued with problems in their conduct toward one another. Paul sets things straight in their understanding of what it is to live a godly life.

2 Corinthians—Paul writes this letter in response to false teachers. He is forced to defend his role as an apostle and helps the Corinthians focus on financially helping the church in Jerusalem.

Galatians—A stunning letter on how Christianity goes beyond Judaism. The role of the law and the role of grace are explored at length.

Ephesians—The mystery of the church is expounded. Paul also gives practical ways for Christians to live in unity while they resist the attacks of demonic forces.

Philippians—Written toward the end of his life, Paul expresses joy in the midst of the hardship of imprisonment. This letter guides Christians in how to deal with overwhelming circumstances.

Colossians—The magnificence of Christ over the Roman emperor Caesar is proclaimed as Paul exposes false philosophies that claim secret knowledge.

1 Thessalonians—Paul encourages young Christians to live godly lives. He also helps us to understand more about the second coming of Christ.

2 Thessalonians—As the Thessalonians were about to suffer greatly under persecution, Paul writes to encourage them to stand strong and gives an end-time perspective to guide them.

1 Timothy—Paul writes to a young minister about how the church is to be organized and run. First Timothy is a primary source for the qualifications of leadership in the church.

2 Timothy—Paul's last known letter before he is killed. He reflects upon the end of his life and encourages Timothy to stay faithful in the midst of false teaching and opposition.

Titus—Paul writes to Titus and gives instructions about leadership in the church. He exhorts Titus to help believers live godly lives and to resist false teaching.

Philemon—A short letter dealing with slavery and the gospel.

Hebrews—Though the author is unknown, this letter shows us how Christ fulfills the requirements of the Jewish law and its regulations.

James—This is the "just do it" letter. James exhorts believers to live out what they hold to in the faith. It is a practical guide for living the Christian life.

1 Peter—The apostle Peter encourages Christians to grow in the faith, trusting in the hope Christ gives us.

2 Peter—Once again dealing with Christian growth, this amazing letter delves into the second coming of Christ.

1 John—The apostle John explains the forgiveness of Christ and the implications of how that affects the way we view ourselves and others.

2 John—Christians are encouraged to love one another and beware of false teachers.

3 John—A short personal letter that deals with the differences between right and wrong motives among leaders.

Jude—Written by Jesus' half brother, Jude makes the point that grace does not mean that Christians can live any way they want to.

The Epistles cover the panorama of human behavior that we often see in churches today. Church splits? Immorality among God's people? Look at the letters to the Corinthians. Strange beliefs, mixing the teachings of Christ with other religions? Colossians becomes our guide. Hypocrites in the congregation? Galatians talks about that. Leaders with wrong motives? You will find that in 1 Timothy. It seems that all the problems we see in our churches today have been around for a while.

This is where we learn to apply the Epistles to our lives. If the problems then were basically the same ones we have today, then the responses that were written to address those problems still apply. For example, here is a warning from Paul about false spirituality among the Colossian Christians:

> Let no one disqualify you, insisting on asceticism and worship of angels, going on in detail about visions, puffed up without reason by his sensuous mind, and not holding fast to the Head, from whom the whole body, nourished and knit together through its joints and ligaments, grows with a growth that is from God.
>
> Colossians 2:18–19

In other words, if spiritual teaching is putting more emphasis upon the teacher than on Christ, something is seriously wrong! Even though there are a lot of stories, be wary of anything that does not put Christ at the center. Following that kind of teaching could disqualify you from the true prize. This is a great description of spiritual pride that applies as much today as it did when this letter was written.

There are many doctrines found in the Epistles. So many, in fact, that there can be a lot of different opinions about what the Epistles actually teach. This is unavoidable, but there are ways to minimize confusion. Here are some general guidelines we can use as we apply truths that are found throughout the Epistles:

Know the "big picture" of Scripture.

This will give you a framework to guide you in understanding passages. Here is the basic plot:

- God created the world and man. It was a beautiful and glorious place.[4]

- Mankind rebelled against God and released a curse upon God's creation, separating man from the Creator.[5]

- God chose a people group whom He would use to display His nature and purposes. These people would provide the seedbed for His plan to bring all of mankind back to himself.[6]

- Because of God's great love for all mankind, He sent Jesus Christ to this people group. Jesus lived the life that man was supposed to live and then gave that life away in death. This death was God's perfect justice—the punishment that all of mankind deserved for their rebellion against God fell upon Jesus, the innocent God/man who should not have died.[7]

- As a result, God raised Jesus Christ from the dead and opened the way to know God. He released the Holy Spirit to His children and expanded the meaning of "the people of God."[8]

- This has started a "new creation"[9] in those who realize that Jesus Christ is alive and now trust in Him for the forgiveness of their sins. This new creation begins in people's hearts as they learn to walk with God again through Christ, and then throughout all the earth as they prepare for Christ's coming again.[10]

- When He comes again, He will judge all of humanity in a new heaven and a new earth. It will be beautiful and glorious—a dwelling place for the Lamb and His bride.[11]

When you understand the eternal plot of the Bible, you can analyze specific epistles in the light of the big picture. You can see Galatians as a response to the growing pains that occur with the adoption of the Gentiles into the promised people. James helps us identify the results of walking in these "new creation" realities. Timothy gives us the guidelines of leadership for this new community. Each epistle has been handpicked by the Holy Spirit to equip us as the people of God.

Take an hour and read an epistle in one sitting.

This is vital if you want to understand the theme of the entire letter. Remember that the chapters and numbers you see in the Bible today were not added until the mid-1500s. These letters were originally designed to be read as one work.

- Think paragraphs. Sometimes the verses were separated in an awkward way. A great example of that is Romans 8:1, which has the greatest impact when seen in the context of Romans 7.
- Make a note of the different parts of an epistle. Each letter has an outline that can guide us. The outline usually follows this pattern:
  - name of the author
  - name of the recipient
  - greeting
  - prayer
  - main points of the letter
  - farewell

Make a distinction between the things that are moral and the things that are cultural.[12]

- Things like adultery, drunkenness, greed, and sexual immorality are *always* wrong.

73

- Things like greeting with a holy kiss, men's hair length, and women's headdress can be seen as cultural.
- A Bible dictionary can help you make these distinctions.

Stay humble as you study the Epistles.

Realize that there will be differences of opinion about certain doctrines. Paul addresses how we should respond to these differences in Romans:

> Accept him whose faith is weak, without passing judgment on disputable matters.
>
> Romans 14:1 NIV1984

Notice the phrase *disputable matters*. There are many practical applications of the Christian life that can be interpreted in a number of ways. When we look past actions and explore motives, we often find common ground. This allows us to accept one another without passing judgment.

As one ancient writer said:

> "Unity in necessary things, liberty in doubtful things, charity in all things."[13]

The Epistles of the New Testament have given the church some of the most beautiful passages in the Bible. They have also exposed us to extremely complex doctrines that we still struggle to understand today. This is a brief introduction on how to read the Epistles. For a list of other books that can take you further along in your understanding of these letters, refer to appendix B.

Summary

The Epistles tell us that the church has had problems from the very beginning, but God uses the problems of the early church to guide us today. Although the Epistles were not intended to cover every issue of life, they are sufficient to give us all that we need to live before God with a clean conscience and to keep the church healthy and flourishing.

CHAPTER 7

The Old Testament Narratives

[As a young Christian] I finished reading the Old Testament in roughly a month, and although I was enjoying the stories, I was confused about how I should understand them.

Mark Driscoll, pastor and author

Let's face it—there are a lot of Christians who avoid the Old Testament (with maybe the exception of the Psalms and Proverbs). The reasoning goes like this: *If we now have the teachings of Jesus Christ, why should we concern ourselves with the Old Testament and its ancient, obsolete laws? What relevance does that part of Scripture have to us today?* These are legitimate questions and will be addressed in this chapter.

Starting in 2005, the British Broadcasting Corporation released a series of nature documentaries using new technology that revolutionized this genre of film making. One of the episodes was set in East Africa, where the film crew captured a small pack of wildebeest roaming the African plains. The dust from their journey swirls around them as we watch the drama of the animals' day-to-day survival. As time progresses, we recognize the leader of the pack and see the complexities of group dynamics.

Then the camera pulls back, and we see other groups of wildebeest moving in the same direction. It becomes apparent that whole herds of wildebeest are in migration. The swirl of dust now looks more like a cloud that comes up from the ground and creates a haze over these unique and beautiful creatures.

The camera pulls back even more. With the ground-breaking use of a camera mounted on a helicopter, we see many different kinds of animals from a stunning height as they make their way through the African Serengeti: not only wildebeest but also zebras and gazelles and other predators, such as leopards and hyenas that move like shadows on the outskirts of this living river of animals. We recognize that they are following an age-old passage to water, and in doing so are ensuring the future of all their species.

Being aware of these multiple perspectives may help us as we look at the accounts of the Old Testament. There are different viewpoints available to us as readers. Each one gives us an important part of the story, and each story tells us something significant about both God and ourselves.

In the first vantage, we see people and places. The story is filled with history and the actions that shape it. There is a young shepherd boy, David, facing a seasoned nine-foot-tall warrior, Goliath.[1] A new leader, Joshua, deals with the responsibility of bringing the Israelites into a land that, though promised, is still unknown to them.[2] Jacob, the deceiver, wrestles with a mysterious man just before he meets his brother Esau for the first time since Jacob stole Esau's birthright.[3] These are emotional and tense accounts of men and women who walked with God in their time.

Our perspective expands as the "camera" widens its focus on the Old Testament: God will display His glory by choosing a people. The story of Jacob is an interesting one from this vantage point. Jacob was born with a natural ability to manipulate everyone around him, especially his family. Why would God bless a deceiver like Jacob, who tricked his brother Esau out of his inheritance? It was because of God's promise to Jacob's grandfather, Abraham, to use his descendants to bless the earth.[4] In a way, the story of Jacob is more about God's purposes than it is about Jacob. This helps us understand why the mystery man (whom we later perceive to be God) approached Jacob to begin with. God chose Jacob; Jacob did not choose God.

Finally, we see a sign of things to come when the camera moves back for a panoramic shot from the heights. The mysterious man is obviously superior to Jacob, and during their wrestling match, the man dislocates Jacob's hip. It seems that Jacob has been seriously injured, but even when he can no longer wrestle, Jacob does what he has always done: He hangs on and asks for a blessing. This is a picture of faith in action. The God figure was so impressed that he declared Jacob the winner and blessed him![5]

As theologian Edmund Clowney states in his wonderful sermon *The Champion's Strange Victory*:

> Jacob certainly did not pin his opponent; his win was hardly a wrestler's victory. He won when he was helpless, he had power with God when his power was gone, and he knew it. . . . Jacob was a winner by grace.[6]

When we regard this account from a panoramic viewpoint, we see that each story of the Old Testament witnesses to God's amazing grace. Grace has been a part of the "big picture" from the garden of Eden onward.

The mysterious wrestler is a figure who will appear later in this great narrative. Where else do we find a powerful being, who sets his vast advantage aside in order to give the victory to someone who is weak and helpless? We could go straight from this account to Paul's description of Jesus Christ:

> Though he was God,
> he did not think of equality with God
> as something to cling to.
> Instead, he gave up his divine privileges,
> he took the humble position of a slave
> and was born as a human being.
>
> Philippians 2:6–7 NLT

As we view the Old Testament in this fashion, we can see that Jesus shows up over and over again. When Paul writes about Jesus being the mediator between God and man,[7] the imagery from the book of Exodus of the cloud by day, the pillar of fire by night, and the burning bush takes on new significance. David and Moses point to someone greater, and to see their storms in this light is revolutionary. There is more to these accounts than meets the eye.

Now we will look at a part of the Old Testament that can discourage many sincere readers: the law of Moses. As we recounted in the introduction, when people get a passion to read the Bible, many start with the book of Genesis.

Genesis gives the account of creation, and the reason why it is so amazing and so corrupt at the same time. The original intent of God for mankind is revealed: God creates the earth for mankind, and mankind for God. Though things go wrong in the beginning, God promises the nomad Abraham that there would be a people who would know Him and walk in His ways in the midst of a broken and rebellious world. The rest of Genesis unfolds in the way God forms this people in the ancient world.

Exodus tells the story of the enslavement of God's people by the Egyptians. God raises up a deliverer named Moses to lead His people out of Egypt, but the Egyptians resist, and God answers with the ten plagues. Exodus also contains the Ten Commandments and instructions for a tent where God would meet His people. This was called the tent of Moses, or the tabernacle.

By the time we get to **Leviticus**, the details become so dense that many readers lose their footing and find that their motivation to read the Bible dries up. Leviticus establishes Jewish identity through the priesthood and festivals. With the number of commands concerning cleanliness and dedication to God, living a life that is pleasing to God becomes a daunting task. Yet Leviticus is filled with gems of wisdom when seen through the work of Christ.

Numbers describes the preparations the Jews undertook to enter the land that God promised them. They come to the border of that land and send in spies, who are overwhelmed by the obstacles they see and bring back a report that the Jews won't survive there. God then forbids this generation of Jews to enter the Promised Land because of their unbelief, and forty years of wandering in the wilderness ensues.

Deuteronomy recounts the speeches that Moses made while the Jews were waiting to go into the Promised Land. There are blessings and curses throughout this book as Moses reminds the nation of Israel to listen to their God and obey His commandments. Deuteronomy ends with the death of Moses and sets the stage for the Israelites to cross the Jordan River. These five books make up what is called the Torah, or the Pentateuch.

There are over six hundred commandments found in the Torah. From dietary laws to clothing, each book is filled with specific guidelines to follow in order to please God. As each new commandment builds upon the other, it seems that the requirements to be a follower of God are impossible to keep up with.

To make it more challenging, Jesus said that not one part of the Law would fade away until there was a new heaven and a new earth.[8]

Then what are Christians to do with the Law? Are we supposed to live according to the laws of the Old Testament? The law of Moses declared many different kinds of animals unclean to eat.[9] You could not plant different seeds in the same field or wear clothing of different fabrics blended into one garment.[10] Do these unusual restrictions still apply to us today?

The first aspect we need to address is that the New Testament by its very name overrides the agreements of the Old Testament. The word *Testament* can also mean "covenant," or "a formal agreement." The Old Testament was God's former binding agreement with the Jewish nation, the New Testament is God's newer (and final) agreement with His creation. Romans 6 gives us some guidance on this:

> For sin will have no dominion over you, since you are not under law but under grace. What then? Are we to sin because we are not under law but under grace? By no means!
>
> Romans 6:14–15 RSV

The apostle Paul is telling the Christians at Rome that the old rules had passed away. New life had come out of the former agreement between God and man. Grace has fulfilled what the law of Moses could not—to call out people from every nation to glorify God from their hearts.

Yet this news didn't start with the New Testament. There are places in the Old Testament that foretell this change. In the midst of great apathy toward God, Jeremiah states:

> "Behold, days are coming," declares the LORD, "when I will make a new covenant with the house of Israel and with the house of Judah, not like the covenant which I made with their fathers in the day I took them by the hand to bring them out of the land of Egypt, My covenant which they broke, although I was a husband to them."
>
> Jeremiah 31:31–32 NASB

When we look at the history of Israel as it is chronicled from Joshua to Esther, we see this pattern.

Joshua—After the death of Moses, Joshua chronicles what happens when the Jewish people inherit the Promised Land. The miracles go from simple survival to how well the Jewish people are willing to obey God in the midst of battle. God meets them as they fight for this new land. It ends with Joshua building an altar of stones to remember God's faithfulness in doing what He promised to do.

Judges—It didn't take long after Joshua's death for the blessing of the land to cause the Israelites to turn their hearts from God to pursue whatever was right in their own eyes. This is a book filled with God's faithfulness to keeping His promises to a people who rebelled at every turn.

Ruth—An unusual narrative of a Moabite widow who experiences the kindness of a Jewish relative, Boaz. With the mandate not to marry outside of Jewish heritage, Ruth's first marriage was a scandal, but God gave Ruth such favor that Boaz redeemed her in Jewish society. Their future offspring would give Israel their most famous king, David, and the Savior of the earth, Jesus Christ.

1 and 2 Samuel—These books are a great study in leadership. They begin with the rise of the prophet Samuel, who in turn grants the Jewish people their request for a king. The first answer to that request is a handsome leader named Saul, the second, a shepherd boy named David. The greatness and failures of these men help to shape the identity of the Jews from a people to a nation.

1 and 2 Kings—Solomon becomes king after David and has a great beginning, but Solomon turns his heart away from God in his later years. After his death, the nation goes into civil war, eventually dividing into Judah and Israel. Both regions continue in their rebellion against God. As a result, God raises up Elijah and Elisha, prophets who will be mouthpieces of God to the abuses of Israel's kings. But even with that, the entire area falls first to the armies of Assyria and then to Babylon.

1 and 2 Chronicles—Probably written as Israel was returning from the Babylonian exile, Chronicles is the "cheat sheet" of Samuel and Kings. It begins with genealogy, goes through Israel's experiences from David up to the Babylonian captivity, and ends with Cyrus, king of Persia, giving the Jews permission to go back to Jerusalem. These books are thought by many to be a quick review of Jewish history to help the returning captives reestablish their cultural identity and renew their confidence as a people, but it is an amazing documentation of God's sovereignty over the affairs of men.

Ezra—Originally combined with Nehemiah, Ezra emphasizes the rebuilding of the temple as the Jews were returning from the Babylonian captivity. As the temple is being rebuilt, Ezra faces opposition from many others, but God gives Ezra favor and the temple is completed.

Nehemiah—Whereas Ezra emphasized rebuilding the temple, Nehemiah emphasizes rebuilding Jerusalem approximately ten years later. Nehemiah demonstrates great leadership as he uses his position as the cupbearer to the Persian king to access the resources and provisions needed for this great task. Nehemiah faces opposition from within his ranks as well as from outside forces, but he stays the course until the wall around Jerusalem is finished. This vital task provides the protection that Jerusalem needed to its infrastructure.

Esther—This story is set just before Ezra and Nehemiah are freed to return to Jerusalem. Esther is a Jewish orphan who has assimilated well into the Persian system, but rises into prominence as she learns of a plot to eradicate the Jews. The book of Esther has all of the elements of a great story—love, conflict, and redemption—but it is the only book in the Bible that makes no mention of God. Esther shows us that God is working even when we are not aware of it.

One thing to note about the history of Israel is that God remains faithful to His purposes even when the Jewish people are constantly being seduced away from Him. It becomes obvious that Israel has not done well in keeping their end of the covenant.

This brings us to one of the reasons another covenant was needed—the first covenant wasn't working. But it never was intended to work by itself. The Old Testament was created to become a pathway to the new covenant in Jesus Christ:

Is the law then contrary to the promises of God? Certainly not! For if a law had been given that could give life, then righteousness would indeed be by the law. But the Scripture imprisoned everything under sin, so that the promise by faith in Jesus Christ might be given to those who believe.

Now before faith came, we were held captive under the law, imprisoned until the coming faith would be revealed. So then, the law was our guardian until Christ came, in order that we might be justified by faith. But now that faith has come, we are no longer under a guardian, for in Christ Jesus you are all sons of God, through faith.

Galatians 3:21–26

The word *guardian* literally meant "a servant who made sure his master's children got to school." In other words, the Law of the Old Testament was crafted to lead God's people to the realization that they could never live up to God's standards. The Israelites (and we) would need a Savior in order to be delivered from the burden of the Law.

If this is the case, and Christ has come, then why do we need to understand the Law at all? There are a number of reasons:

- Even though much of the Old Testament Law was not directed toward us, it is still the words of God. We learn much about the nature and character of a relationship with God from the law of Moses. For example, when we learn about the Tent of Meeting, we learn that there is an outer court, an inner court, and a place called the Holy of Holies.[11]

  What a wonderful picture of how we often approach God in our personal devotions: We are on a journey from the outer court into the Holy Place. Each court is filled with amazing symbols (the need of blood for cleansing, oil for anointing, lamps for His light, and many more) that help us grasp what a relationship with God can be like.

- Jesus said that the Law would not pass away until this heaven and earth are gone. Does that mean that we are still obligated to the Law? No, it means that the Law cannot be changed. It is a constant reminder that we cannot please God by our own efforts. This should lead us to praise and humility, for what the Law could not do, God himself did. Jesus Christ came onto the earth to fulfill *all* of the requirements of the Law that would condemn us

86

to death. Outside of Christ, all of the standards that God revealed to Moses still stand.

When you read the Old Testament, you will find that signposts to grace were always there in God's dealings with His people. The God of judgment in the Old Testament is the same God that is in the New Testament. There was no change in God. It is humankind that keeps turning away from God and suffering disastrous results.

When we understand this, we grasp that the accounts of the Old Testament record God's intervention into the affairs of men rather than merely telling moral stories. The Old Testament does not condone the actions of the people whose stories it contains as much as it documents them for our benefit.

For an example, look at something like polygamy, which was a social institution of the ancient world. If anything, the effects of polygamy in the Old Testament are a picture of chaos and pain. That God blesses David, or his son Solomon, is more a statement of God's faithfulness to His promises than an endorsement of polygamy. As time goes on, we see a steady shift from kings with numerous wives to the requirement that a New Testament leader be the "husband of one wife."[12]

There are also parts of the Old Testament that Jesus validates and expands in the New Testament. In Matthew 5, Jesus gives us a radical new perspective on the commands of Moses. When a teacher of the Law wants to know how to inherit eternal life, Jesus shows him that the Shema, or the Jewish confession of faith, sums up the entire Old Testament.

"Hear, O Israel, the LORD our God, the LORD is one. And you shall love the LORD your God with all your heart, with all your soul, with all your mind, and with all your strength." This is the first commandment. And the second, like it, is this: "You shall love your neighbor as yourself." There is no other commandment greater than these.

So the scribe said to Him, "Well said, Teacher. You have spoken the truth, for there is one God, and there is no other but He. And to love Him with all the heart, with all the understanding, with all the soul, and with all the strength, and to love one's neighbor as oneself, is more than all the whole burnt offerings and sacrifices."

Now when Jesus saw that he answered wisely, He said to him, "You are not far from the kingdom of God."

Mark 12:29–34 NKJV

There are many places in the New Testament that reference passages in the Old Testament. As you see these, take time to look at the original Scriptures. You'll be amazed at how the New Testament authors saw a direct link between the Old Testament and what they were experiencing in their walk with Christ.

Like the Great Migration of the Serengeti, the characters of the Old Testament were on a journey. As the writer of Hebrews declares:

All these people died still believing what God had promised them. They did not receive what was promised, but they saw it all from a distance and welcomed it. They agreed that they were foreigners and nomads here on earth. Obviously people who say such things are looking forward to a country they can call their own. If they had longed for the country they came from, they could have gone back. But they were looking for a better place, a heavenly homeland. That is why God is not ashamed to be called their God, for he has prepared a city for them.

Hebrews 11:13–16 NLT

These men and women were leading all of us to the source of living water—Jesus Christ. And because they were like us, the accounts of their lives are filled with treasures that instruct us on our own journey. In many ways the Old Testament accounts can help us deal with the drama that occurs in our personal lives, for just as God chose these pilgrims for His purposes, He has chosen us as well.

For example, in Genesis we see the ravages of Jacob's bad parenting. His obsession with his wife Rachel caused him to lavish his attention upon her firstborn, Joseph, which caused the sons from his first wife, Leah, to seethe with jealousy. Jacob's gift to Joseph of a colorful coat and Joseph's dream that his brothers would bow to him become the tipping points. Now his brothers feel justified in their plot to get rid of him.[13] Yet God would use this family injustice for His glory when Joseph leads one of the greatest hunger relief efforts in ancient history. Joseph shows us that God can redeem even the most painful family strife.

The Old Testament is filled with stories of people who faced hardship. Their lives reflect the same disappointments and setbacks that you and I face today. But their lives are more than examples of the human experience; there was coming a day when God himself would experience the pain and heartbreak of a fallen world. Hebrews once again helps us to see the importance of this knowledge of Jesus Christ:

> We don't have a priest who is out of touch with our reality. He's been through weakness and testing, experienced it all—all but the sin. So let's walk right up to him and get what he is so ready to give. Take the mercy, accept the help.
>
> Hebrews 4:15–16 The Message

If we could see our lives from a higher vantage point, we would see that God takes the circumstances of our lives and sums all things up in Christ. The Old Testament stands as a witness to that.

May you find a guide in the narrative of the chosen people that will lead you to Christ. Each account is there to help you understand more about God as well as more about yourself.

Summary

The Old Testament is a treasure chest of information about God and about us. As we study the Old Testament, we recognize that without His help, there is no way we could get to know Him. Yet His grace has been there all along—from the making of animal coverings in the garden of Eden to when He saved His people through a Persian king. God has been summing up all things in Christ from the very beginning of time.

CHAPTER 8

Moses: The Man Who Saw God Face-to-Face

The Israelites in Egypt

The descendants of Abraham flourished, and a major famine caused them to seek refuge in Egypt. Under the political protection of the Egyptian Pharaoh, a small band of twelve brothers grew into a people who "multiplied so greatly that they became extremely powerful and filled the land."[1] Their great numbers and power became a political concern for a new Pharaoh who knew little about the Israelites and how they had come to Egypt to begin with.

The fear of a revolt caused the Egyptian government to crack down on the Hebrew people. First, the Egyptians made them slaves, and then the Israelites were assigned the messy and demeaning business of brickmaking. Yet even under increasing oppression, the Israelites continued to grow in numbers as an ethnic group. This alarmed the Egyptian Pharaoh so much that he mandated infanticide in an attempt to limit their numbers and strength. Every male baby was to be drowned in the Nile River. This was the society that Moses was born into.

We know very little about Moses' parents. They were of the house of Levi, and were able to hide the birth of their son in the midst of this dangerous environment. After three months, however, they realized that they could not protect him any longer. So they put their baby son in a papyrus basket and floated him down the Nile River toward one of Pharaoh's daughters as she was bathing in the river.

The irony in this account is stunning. The Nile was the river that Pharaoh used to destroy all the Hebrew male babies, yet the Nile also became the vehicle of Moses' deliverance. In addition, Moses was rescued by one of the daughters of the man who issued his death warrant. It seems that God is not limited by circumstances or resources; God turned this situation on its head.

The inner conflict of growing up as a Hebrew in the Egyptian court was probably immense. Moses was aware of his ethnic heritage. He probably had to endure the comments and humor of his Egyptian peers that came at the Jews' expense. This tension came to a climax as the adult Moses watched an Egyptian beat a Hebrew slave. In a moment of passion, Moses killed the Egyptian and quickly became a fugitive, barely escaping into the wilderness with his life as Pharaoh hunted him and his own people branded him as a troublemaker. The fire within Moses caused him to take revenge into his own hands. Now he was running for his life, but Moses was about to learn how to be an activist God's way.

The Burning Bush

Moses must have felt that life as he knew it was over. This is a common thread in the stories of people in the Bible: a major disappointment is followed by grief over real loss, adjustment to their new realities, and finally, understanding God's purpose for those circumstances. Moses found himself in the desert, learning the skills of a shepherd in a predominantly female family. This was humiliating to a man trained as a royal warrior—and that was exactly what God intended for Moses. God molded him into a man who would not trust in his pedigree or his power, but only in God.

Forty years had passed when Moses encountered a burning bush in the desert. Brush fires were a common sight, but this bush was not consumed by the fire. It was unusual enough to cause Moses to turn aside to take a closer look.

We often expect an encounter with God to be dramatic, and many of them are, but the Bible also describes interactions between God and humanity as so disarming that people are unaware they are in the presence of God. One of Moses' ancestors, Jacob, said after one such encounter, "Surely the LORD is in this place, and I did not know it."[2] Our views of human interactions with God have sometimes been shaped more by Hollywood than by the biblical accounts. Moses' unexpected encounter can also give us insight into why, over one thousand years later, the people of Galilee would not have seen Jesus as anyone special while he was growing up.

God told Moses that the cries of the Hebrews suffering under slavery had risen up to Him and that He had chosen Moses to deliver them out of slavery. By this time Moses had lost his self-confidence to the point that he couldn't speak well in front of others. He argued his unfitness for the role of deliverer, and God became angry with Moses for being reluctant to believe that He could use a broken shepherd. Eventually, Moses came around, and with his brother, Aaron, he set out to confront the most powerful military leader of that time.

Plagues

Things got worse before they got better. Moses demanded that Pharaoh let God's people worship Him on a mountain, and Pharaoh responded by doubling their workload. This was confusing to the people, who had been told they had God's favor, but God had a purpose they couldn't see. The Israelites just wanted to get out of Egypt, but God wanted to prepare them to walk with Him in the Promised Land. Moses' repeated demand and Pharaoh's resistance prompted God's intervention through ten plagues that affected the entire Egyptian empire while bypassing the Hebrews.

The final plague was the most dramatic and paved the way for another divine intervention hundreds of years later. The LORD came through Egypt and killed every firstborn male in the Egyptian empire. In order for the Hebrews to be delivered from God's judgment, they had to perform a specific set of actions.

Each Jewish family took a spotless lamb, slaughtered it, and spread the blood on the doorposts of their home. The Lord saw the blood on the doorposts and passed over that house. This is why the Jewish holiday celebrating the deliverance of Israel is called Passover today.

Passover holds an even greater significance for Christians. According to the New Testament, we all deserve God's judgment for our rebellion against God and His ways, but God provided a lamb to be slaughtered in our place: Jesus Christ. The blood that Jesus shed at the cross is spread upon the doorposts of a new life with God. God will pass over the sin of those who realize that Jesus' death and resurrection is the pathway to God's favor in their lives. The story of the deliverance of the Hebrews from Egypt is also the story of our deliverance from sin, as God's judgment against sin and provision for mercy meet at the cross.

The Jewish rabbi and New Testament writer Paul alludes to the Passover when he writes about his personal journeys:

> Indeed, we felt that we had received the sentence of death. But that was to make us rely not on ourselves but on God who raises the dead. He delivered us from such a deadly peril, and he will deliver us. On him we have set our hope that he will deliver us again.
>
> 2 Corinthians 1:9–10

The Red Sea

The final plague broke the will of Pharaoh, who at last allowed the Israelites to leave Egypt in order to worship their God. But in a stunning move, God had them camp by the Sea of Reeds in such a way that Pharaoh thought the Hebrews were lost in the wilderness and therefore could easily be enslaved again. He sent an army to ambush them.

With the dust of the approaching Egyptian army visible on the horizon, Moses and the Israelites knew that they were on the verge of a massacre. Yet as Moses raised his staff, the waters of the sea parted and the nation of Israel crossed through the sea on a corridor of dry land. This miracle would not deter the Egyptians, for they pursued the Israelites into the sea as well. Once the Hebrew people had passed through, Moses raised his staff again and the waters came crashing down upon the

Egyptian army, freeing the Jewish people from the bonds of Egypt forever.

You would think that the former slaves would now be convinced that God was with them, but that is not what the Bible shows. Just three days later, they complained about having no water, and then they complained about having no meat. This behavior continued through the rest of their time in the wilderness.

There are many people today who think that if only they saw a miracle, they would believe that God exists, but that is not what the Bible teaches. The Israelites saw some of the greatest miracles ever witnessed, and within three days they felt abandoned by God. The issue is not what is going on outside of our lives, but what is happening inside our hearts. The Israelites remind us that the entrance into God's kingdom is not by amazing feats of supernatural power, but by quietly humbling our hearts before God.

Moses' Leadership

After setting up civic courts to keep order among the people, the Lord led Moses and the Jewish people to Mount Sinai. God met Moses there and gave him the laws that would define the Israelites as the people of God. The best known of these laws are the Ten Commandments, but there were many more laws established at this time. Festivals were prescribed to be observed every year. God gave specific instructions on how to build a place of worship, called the tabernacle. God revealed a new identity to the Israelites that was radically different from the one they had in Egypt. They were no longer slaves; they were the people of God living in the freedom to celebrate who God made them to be.

These encounters with God were transformative for Moses, so much so that he had to wear a veil, because the glory of God's presence radiated from his face. Moses' sin had taken him from the courts of Pharaoh to the desert, but God transformed him from a broken shepherd to a powerful leader. Moses had always been an activist; now God had prepared him to bring change God's way instead of his own.

Like Abraham, Moses did not do things perfectly. At one point, Moses discovered that the Israelites were worshiping a golden calf that they had made while he was on Mount Sinai with God. Their idolatry made Moses so angry that he smashed the stone tablets on which God himself had written His laws. In another incident, Moses' anger caused God to forbid his entering the Promised Land.

In spite of all of this, Moses was a humble man. When people questioned his leadership, Moses leaned upon the Lord to validate his position. Moses inherited the blessing of Abraham. It is estimated that the population of the freed Jews was around two million.[3] They were as numerous as the sand in the sea and stars in the sky, but the burden of leading them would cause Moses to ask God to kill him.[4]

It actually gets worse.

As they came near the Promised Land, Moses sent twelve spies ahead to scout out the area. Instead of simply giving a report about the land, ten of the spies told the Israelites there was no way they could take the land because the tribes in that area were too strong.

This was not what Moses expected. Instead of giving information that would build their confidence to enter the Promised Land, the spies spread so much fear among the Israelites that they decided not to enter at all. Therefore, God mandated that this generation would wander in the wilderness until they died.

God wanted a people who would obey Him in the Promised Land, not wither at every obstacle. Moses would now be their leader in the wilderness for forty years, protecting a vision that he would never personally see.

Dying to Our Own Agendas

The blessing of the Lord is not a way out of pressure or responsibility. On the contrary, we find that God's blessing will put us in situations where we need God's help more than ever. As we look at the journey of Moses, we see a man who was willing (sometimes reluctantly) to take on responsibilities that were challenging, to say the least. As he did, however, God formed him into a great deliverer and leader. The story of Moses shows us that God is more interested in what we become than in what we do.

Paul once again brings insight on the way God guides us when he writes:

> We are hard pressed on every side, but not crushed; perplexed, but not in despair; persecuted, but not abandoned; struck down, but not destroyed. We always carry around in our body the death of Jesus, so that the life of Jesus may also be revealed in our body. For we who are alive are always being given over to death for Jesus' sake, so that his life may be revealed in our mortal body. So then, death is at work in us, but life is at work in you.
>
> 2 Corinthians 4:8–12 NIV

Moses had to die to his own agenda in order for God's purpose to be fulfilled. That may seem difficult, but the results speak for themselves. He became one of the greatest liberators in history, and in so doing established the nation that began with Abraham. God made Moses into the strong leader he was meant to be.

In the same way, when we are willing to die to our own agenda and listen to what God is saying in His Word, we too can receive a life far greater than the one we have manufactured for ourselves. God is taking us from glory to glory, and He has given us Moses' example to show us the realities of what that journey looks like.

CHAPTER 9

Poetry in the Bible

> Poetry provides the one permissible way of saying one thing and meaning another.... We like to talk in parables and in hints and in indirections.
>
> Robert Frost

'll never forget the time we had a presentation of photographic art for one of the initial services of our fledgling church in Manhattan. We were meeting monthly in a local high school auditorium and were excited about using the arts as a vehicle for communicating God's truth to our community.

A photographer put together a presentation of more than two hundred abstract photos that moved at a rate of one photo per second, creating a unique sense of movement. The purpose was to tell the story of the beauty of God's creation, the fall of that creation, and the ultimate restoration of all things. As each photo flashed before our eyes to the rhythm of ethereal music, I felt very proud that we were showing this in our church. It was cutting edge and avant-garde. *We* were cutting edge and avant-garde.

But as we left the service, one of our members, a well-educated professional, turned to me rather sheepishly and said, "Pastor Dave, I have to admit that I didn't understand what that presentation meant. I'm sorry, but I just didn't get it." His candor helped me to realize that in my attempt to be artsy, I hadn't prepared the congregation well enough for what they were about to see. As a result, the impact of the presentation was lost on many of our people.

In a similar way, one of our congregants, who happens to be a writer, invited a number of his friends from church to a reading night in his neighborhood. Held at a local establishment, a dozen budding authors took turns reading their work over a microphone. Some were profound. Some addressed mature themes. Some were poetry.

The next morning I met with one of the attendees of the reading night. As he described the evening to me, he said, "Of all that was read, I didn't understand the poetry. I tried really hard, but I didn't get it."

Poetry is like that. Most of us don't get it at first. In our early school years, we learn how words rhyme, but for the most part we see poetry as song lyrics written to fit a beat. We read Shakespeare in school, but the language seems so foreign, we try to avoid it rather than work to understand what it means. The robust sale of CliffsNotes and other study guides tells us how much we don't like to wrestle with words.

However, the Bible is filled with poetry. The Psalms were crafted as poems to be sung. The Proverbs are short lines of poetry that were meant to give us nuggets of wisdom about life (though some of them cause us to scratch our heads in confusion). The Song of Solomon has poetic imagery that, if we understood it, would make us blush at its sexual candor. Poems are scattered throughout both the Old and New Testaments.

If we believe Scripture is divinely inspired, what do we do with the poetry? Why is Scripture filled with it? These are legitimate questions that we will be exploring in this chapter, but because most people don't read poetry, we first need to talk about why it is useful. If we don't understand the nature of poetry, we can become easily confused about what biblical poetry is saying. Interestingly enough, the non-poetic parts of the Bible help frame the role of poetry and why God uses it to reveal himself to humankind.

The apostle John was exiled to the island of Patmos because he upset the Romans with his proclamations about Jesus being the true God. But the Romans who banished him couldn't stop the work of God. John had one more book to write, and it has become one of the most famous and controversial books in the Bible: the book of Revelation. At the beginning of this work, John describes an experience that sets the tone for the rest of the book:

> Then I turned to see the voice that was speaking to me, and on turning I saw seven golden lampstands, and in the midst of the lampstands one *like* a son of man, clothed with a long robe and with a golden sash around his chest. The hairs of his head were white, *like* white wool, *like* snow. His eyes were *like* a flame of fire, his feet were *like* burnished bronze, refined in a furnace, and his voice was *like* the roar of many waters. In his right hand he held seven stars, from his mouth came a sharp two-edged sword, and this face was *like* the sun shining in full strength.
>
> Revelation 1:12–16, emphasis added

Notice that John describes this vision in approximations—the figure's eyes are *like* a flame of fire. In other words, John can't quite grasp what he is seeing, so he uses imagery that comes as close as possible to describing what he is experiencing. This supernatural being is too much for words—John can't use exact language to catch the moment. This parallels a similar experience that Daniel recorded:

> And in the four and twentieth day of the first month, as I was by the side of the great river, which is Hiddekel, then I lifted up mine eyes, and looked, and behold a certain man clothed in linen, whose loins were girded with fine gold of Uphaz: His body also was *like* the beryl, and his face *as* the appearance of lightning, and his eyes *as* lamps of fire, and his arms and his feet *like* in colour to polished brass, and the voice of his words *like* the voice of a multitude.
>
> Daniel 10:4–6 KJV, emphasis added

One of the recurring themes of Scripture is that there are things about God and His heavenly realm that can't be fully captured by language. This is where it can get confusing: the Scripture is very clear about God and His works on the earth, but in that clarity we see that God is beyond the descriptions of Him. In a sense, exact communication is not enough to capture who He really is.[1]

This is where poetry comes in. It has mystery, double meanings, and a certain vagueness that can create imagery beyond the words it uses—and that is the point. In the Psalms, we read of God as a warrior with smoke coming out of His nostrils, and who fires arrows,[2] yet He is also depicted as a rock.[3] There are mountains singing and trees clapping their hands,[4] and people standing secure on the heights with feet like deer.[5] The metaphors expand our perspective about God and how we can know and experience Him.

When we look at the world through this understanding of God, we see that life is not a dry dissertation that fits neatly into categories for analysis. The biblical picture presents life as a poem: rich, mysterious, and passionate. Maybe this is one reason why we are so moved by the arts, whether in words, images, or sounds. Could it be that the reason why there is so much poetry in the Bible is because God created us to respond to this kind of language?

Poetry is also easier to memorize. We will talk much more about the role of prophetic literature in the Bible in the next chapter, but when people in the ancient world wanted to remember something, they created a poem about it. It is no wonder that the classic works of the ancient world that have endured the test of time—such as *The Odyssey* and *The Iliad*—are epic poems.

There is so much poetry in the Bible that breaking it down by books may be the easiest way to see how it is used. This is just an introduction, and there are many other ways to understand biblical poetry, but for our purposes, let's look at the Psalms, Proverbs, the Prophets, and the New Testament.

The Psalms

Think about the popularity of the Psalms over the centuries. The picture painted in Psalm 23 of a shepherd leading his sheep to green pastures and still waters has been a source of comfort to people for generations. This imagery communicates so fully to us that we may fail to realize how vague the language of the Psalms is.

For example, Psalm 1 NKJV:

> Blessed is the man
> Who walks not in the counsel of the ungodly,
>> Nor stands in the path of sinners,
>> Nor sits in the seat of the scornful,

But his delight is in the law of the LORD,
   And in His law he meditates day and night.
He shall be like a tree
   Planted by the rivers of water,
   That brings forth its fruit in its season,
   Whose leaf also shall not wither,
   And whatever he does shall prosper.

The ungodly are not so,
But are like the chaff which the wind drives away.
Therefore the ungodly shall not stand in the judgment,
Nor sinners in the congregation of the righteous.

For the LORD knows the way of the righteous,
But the way of the ungodly shall perish.

This Psalm was written at a time when water was not so easily accessible, so the metaphor of a tree always bearing fruit is a sharp contrast to chaff, which is basically a waste product. These agricultural references are not a part of most of our life experiences in the twenty-first century, yet the imagery is so clear and simple that it still speaks to us today. We long to be people who are always productive. We want to live lives blessed by God.

However, the vagueness of the words used opens the door to many different applications. Notice the progression that starts the Psalm: walking with the ungodly, standing where sinners walk, and then sitting with cynical people. This is in contrast to being planted in God's Word. The first three are openly seen, whereas planting is underground—an internal posture. We could speak of walking in terms of how we set goals, standing in terms of where we position ourselves for understanding, and sitting in terms of those with whom we identify ourselves. The multiple meanings of poetry produce a treasure chest of insights.

Now let's look at how poetry can be misunderstood. Psalm 51 was written to express David's repentance for committing adultery with Uriah's wife, Bathsheba. His lament is strongly emotional. In verse 5 (NASB) he states:

> Behold, I was brought forth in iniquity,
> And in sin my mother conceived me.

Gordon Fee and Douglas Stuart bring strong insight to this passage:

> [David] is hardly trying to establish the doctrine that conception is sinful, or that all conceptions are sinful, or that his mother was a sinner by getting pregnant, or that original sin applies to unborn children, or any such thing. The psalmist has employed hyperbole—purposeful exaggeration—in order to express strongly and vividly that he is a sinner.[6]

Once again, this is the role of poetry. It is a medium made to express things in unusual terms so that we can arrive at a deeper truth. As a result, the book of Psalms is not the place to establish doctrine, though the Psalms are rich with doctrinal insight. The Psalms are honest and emotional expressions of prayer to God that give us full permission to be just as honest when we pray.

This raw emotion is displayed in Psalm 137, where the Israelites are mourning their captivity by the Babylonians. Verses 8 and 9 provide a jarring ending:

> O daughter of Babylon, doomed to be destroyed,
> blessed shall he be who repays you
> with what you have done to us!
> Blessed shall he be who takes your little ones
> and dashes them against the rock!

To think that this passage condones something unimaginable is wrong and misses the point. The psalmist had such a freedom in his relationship with God that he was able to express the pain of what he had witnessed. Ephesians 4:26 states, "In your anger, do not sin," but this is an anger that is diverted from men to God, who is the only being who can righteously handle that anger. The Psalms invite us to express the vast range of human emotion in our relationship with God. With a straightforward portrayal of the passion that we all experience in our souls, the Psalms show us that the greatest way to know God is to be fully human.

The Proverbs

The Proverbs are a part of what many scholars call the "Wisdom Literature" of the Bible, which consists of Proverbs, the Song of Solomon, Ecclesiastes, and Job. The purpose of the Wisdom Literature is to guide us toward what it means to live "the good life." Many cultures have a set of proverbs that they aspire to live by.

Look at this passage in Proverbs 3:

> Trust GOD from the bottom of your heart,
> don't try to figure out everything on your own.
> Listen for GOD'S voice in everything you do, every-
> where you go,
> he's the one who will keep you on track.
> Don't assume that you know it all.
> Run to GOD! Run from evil!
> Your body will glow with health,
> your very bones will vibrate with life!
>
> vv. 5–8 THE MESSAGE

"Trust in the LORD . . ." It is this emphasis that makes the Wisdom Literature of the Bible stand apart from other religions; wisdom does not begin with us, it begins with God.

The Proverbs were specifically written in short, catchy phrases that would stick in one's memory. Just like advertisers use slogans that are quickly associated with their product, the Proverbs were crafted as sound bites to instruct us in what to do in the moment.

This is what makes the Proverbs so effective. Look at Proverbs 6:

> Take a lesson from the ants, you lazybones.
> Learn from their ways and become wise!
> Though they have no prince
> or governor or ruler to make them work,
> they labor hard all summer,
> gathering food for the winter.
>
> Proverbs 6:6–8 NLT

Does this mean that we don't need supervisors? No. This Proverb addresses how to be proactive. Many times we wait for someone to tell us what to do, but look at the way of the ant. Instead of only doing the bare minimum, start asking, "What needs to happen next?" The next thing you know, you will see resources increase and provisions arrive when you need them. Sometimes we wait on God to do something, while God is waiting on us to do something.

The last passage brings us to another important aspect about Proverbs: They were not written to be applicable in every situation. They are short and meant to have a limited use. Once again, Proverbs 6 is not a doctrinal stance for maverick work ethics. Rather, the application is about diligence and its benefits.

The poetry and brevity of Proverbs creates a very effective way to remember ways to live your life before God. Just like the Psalms, they are not meant to be sources of doctrine so much as perspectives on the application of God's Word to our lives.

Ecclesiastes

Ecclesiastes is a unique book in the Bible. The very beginning will tell you that to the one without a healthy perspective on life, everything is meaningless:

> "Meaningless! Meaningless!"
> says the Teacher.
> "Utterly meaningless!
> Everything is meaningless."
> Ecclesiastes 1:2 NIV

Normally associated with Solomon, the son of King David, the rest of the book stays true to this theme. From the perspective of a man who has it all—money, power, fame—it seems like no matter what is achieved in this life, death will claim everything in the end. Ecclesiastes is cynical to the core.

And that is the beauty of the book.

Solomon basically asks, "What if God didn't exist?" He then brilliantly describes a place that would bring anyone to a point of despair. Centuries before atheists like Richard Dawkins or Christopher Hitchens were born, Solomon told us that if there were no God, there would be no purpose except what we make up for ourselves. To the honest person, this would be unsatisfying, to say the least.

At this point you may be asking, "Then why is this book in the Bible at all?" One answer could be God's love for all humanity. Think of it this way: If God wanted to reveal himself to all creation, wouldn't it make sense to include a book that would communicate His truth to the cynic? This is what Ecclesiastes gives us. If this book is a highway to fatalism, the last two verses of the book provide an exit ramp to the rest of the Bible:

The end of the matter, all has been heard.
Fear God, and keep his commandments,
for this is the whole duty of man.
For God will bring every deed into judgment,
with every secret thing, whether good or evil.
Ecclesiastes 12:13–14 RSV

Ecclesiastes brings credibility to the claim that the Scriptures are God's words to *all* humanity.

The Song of Solomon

The Song of Solomon is a love story depicting a young couple consummating their marriage. Though some people see this as an allegory for the church, this is not the main intent. The symbolism within this song speaks of sexual delight within marriage that should not be sanitized or ignored.

In a sexually charged culture like we have today, it should be comforting to know that God is not silent on the topic. The Bible acknowledges sexual desire as one of the strongest human urges. So strong, in fact, that it takes the strength of a covenant between a man and a woman to keep sex from becoming a harsh taskmaster over our souls. No wonder this love song states three times,

Don't excite love, don't stir it up,
until the time is ripe—and you're ready.
Song of Songs 2:7; 3:5; 8:4
THE MESSAGE

The Song of Songs affirms that our physical life is not bad—it is good, but fallen. To keep sex for marriage is not a puritanical restraint; it is a safeguard to give us the full satisfaction that God intended for sex. The Song of Songs is a lampstand to the ravages of the sexual revolution and calls us back to the abundant life God created us for.

Job

Scholars are divided about when the book of Job was written. Some say it is the oldest book of the Bible to be written (from 2000 BC to 1600 BC) while others think it could have been written during the time of Solomon (from 600 BC to 450 BC). No matter what time period we place on this ancient text, Job deals with the most difficult reality we face: pain and suffering. Job is depicted as a righteous man who has to endure incredible suffering for no apparent reason, except that Satan challenges God about the true motives of His servants.

The book of Job basically asks the question "Why do bad things happen to good people?" and then proceeds to give us all the wrong answers.

For the next thirty-nine chapters, we see Job's friends grasp for the meaning of suffering. Many of their critiques of Job would sound familiar to many of us today: Job is suffering because he did something wrong, because this pain must be a warning from God, or because Job must be hiding something. Instead of trying to justify himself, Job takes his complaints to God. When God confronts Job in chapter 40 with a creation that is bigger than anything Job can fathom, Job turns his complaints into worship. In the end, God is angry with Job's friends for trying to fit suffering into a formula. This profound book leaves us with God blessing Job with more than he had before, but never answering the age-old question of why pain exists.

The poetry of Job is awe-inspiring. Many nonreligious scholars regard Job as one of the greatest literary works of all time.

Job challenges us to reconcile two seemingly contradictory truths: life is unfair, but God is good. The world is not what it is supposed to be, and Job stands as a witness to how we are to respond. As Job realized, if he is allowed to get mad at a God who could stop suffering but doesn't, then Job must also concede that God could be great enough to have a reason for pain and suffering that we will not understand this side of heaven. The proper response is to trust God.

The Poetry of the Prophets

As we begin to see the role of poetry, we can see the reason why the prophets used it a lot. In a culture that placed a high value on memorization, poetry was a powerful way to communicate the heart of God to an obstinate people.

Look at the vision Isaiah gives us in poetic form:

> Hear, O heavens, and give ear, O earth:
> for the LORD hath spoken,
> I have nourished and brought up children,
> and they have rebelled against me.
> The ox knoweth his owner, and the ass his master's
>   crib:
> but Israel doth not know,
> my people doth not consider.
>
> Isaiah 1:2–3 KJV

Through the poetic use of metaphor, even if we have never owned an ox or a donkey, we get a picture of what God wants to address among His people. This usage of metaphor is a pattern in much of the poetry used by the prophets.

Hosea was a prophet in Northern Israel during a time when the national leadership was rebellious to God and His ways.

The poetry of Hosea uses the metaphor of a husband who has an adulterous wife:

> I will not show my love to her children,
> because they are the children of adultery.
> Their mother has been unfaithful
> and has conceived them in disgrace.
> She said, "I will go after my lovers,
> who give me my food and my water,
> my wool and my linen, my oil and my drink."
>
> Hosea 2:4–5 NIV

The imagery is striking. Israel has become unfaithful through her leaders, and the people are suffering for their leaders' rebellion. Yet throughout this passionate poetic discourse, there are calls to return to God and be healed. Hosea gives us dramatic understanding of a God who is committed to restore a people who are determined to rebel against Him. But God's determination is greater than Israel's. At the end of Hosea, God states:

> I will heal their waywardness
> and love them freely,
> for my anger has turned away from them.
> I will be like the dew to Israel,
> he will blossom like a lily.
> Like a cedar of Lebanon
> he will send down his roots,
> his young shoots will grow.
> His splendor will be like an olive tree,
> his fragrance like a cedar of Lebanon.
> Men will dwell again in his shade.
> He will flourish like the grain.
> He will blossom like a vine,
> and his fame will be like the wine from Lebanon.
>
> Hosea 14:4–7 NIV

Hosea is filled with emotion. The venting of anger, the pain of rejection, and the calls to repentance are fully captured in this book. The depth of the sins committed illuminate the height of God's great love, and without poetry, we would be lacking in our understanding of both realities.

Poetry in the New Testament

With such a heritage of poetry in the Old Testament, it should come as no surprise that the New Testament has many instances of poetry and poetic influences as well. When the young pregnant Mary sees her cousin Elizabeth, she breaks into a beautiful poem called "The Magnificat."

> My soul magnifies the Lord,
> And my spirit has rejoiced in God my Savior.
> For He has regarded the lowly state of His maidservant,
> For behold, henceforth all generations will call me
> blessed.
> For He who is mighty has done great things for me,
> And holy is His name.
> And His mercy is on those who fear Him
> From generation to generation.
> He has shown strength with His arm,
> He has scattered the proud in the imagination of their
> hearts.
> He has put down the mighty from their thrones,
> And exalted the lowly.
> He has filled the hungry with good things,
> And the rich He has sent away empty.
> He has helped His servant Israel,
> In remembrance of His mercy,
> As He spoke to our fathers,
> To Abraham and to his seed forever.
>
> Luke 1:46–55 NKJV

In a similar way, the apostle Paul tells the church at Ephesus:

Be filled with the Spirit, speaking to one another in psalms and hymns and spiritual songs, singing and making melody with your heart to the Lord, always giving thanks for all things.

Ephesians 5:18–20 NASB

One of these hymns can be found in 1 Timothy:

Great indeed, we confess, is the mystery of godliness:
He was manifested in the flesh,
vindicated by the Spirit,
seen by angels,
proclaimed among the nations,
believed on in the world,
taken up in glory.

1 Timothy 3:16

The church has such a rich musical heritage that polyphony (singing and playing in harmony) and notation (written music) are attributed to Christianity. The Old Testament poetic sensibilities are found throughout the New Testament. Philippians 3 displays a rhythm that connects us directly to Hebraic poetry. Paul even quotes Greek poetry to the leading thinkers of Greece while he shares the gospel with them.[7] It seems that poetry is more evident in the New Testament than we recognize at first.

In one of the more dramatic poetic moments of the New Testament, Paul writes about the instant in which every believer in Jesus Christ shall be transformed:

When the perishable puts on the imperishable, and the mortal puts on immortality, then shall come to pass the saying that is written:

116

"Death is swallowed up in victory."
"O death, where is your victory?
O death, where is your sting?"
The sting of death is sin, and the power of sin is the law. But thanks be to God, who gives us the victory through our Lord Jesus Christ.

1 Corinthians 15:54–57

Not only is God so great that we need the language of poetry to describe Him accurately, but we also face a future that is so great it is best captured through the poetic. God has given us poetry in the Scripture to help us understand Him and ourselves with greater depth and clarity.

Summary

The truth about God is so glorious that it can't be captured in a direct way, thus the Bible is filled with poetry. Poetry uses ambiguity to unveil different meanings in the same writing. It is also easier to memorize. Poetry ministers to us in a powerful way through the seasons of life, for what we miss during one period of life can impact us in another.

CHAPTER 10

David: A Man After God's Own Heart

Samuel Seeks a New King

What ran through the mind of the young shepherd boy David when he heard that the prophet Samuel wanted to see him? The renowned man of God had made a surprise visit to Bethlehem, and then issued a personal invitation to David's father, Jesse, to join him for a meal. That must have been quite a shock to the family of shepherds, but David would not be able to participate. Someone had to watch the sheep, and as the youngest son, David dutifully took care of the family business while his brothers joined their father. But then a messenger came to David in the field—David was being summoned to join his family and the great prophet for the sacrifice.

The elders of Bethlehem had been gripped by fear when Samuel first arrived in their little town. Saul, the current king of Israel, had dishonored the Lord once again. This time it was blatant disobedience to the Lord's commands during a strategic

119

military campaign. Saul had publicly insulted Samuel by offering a sacrifice to God without the prophet, which was forbidden according to the laws God had given through Moses.

A national spectacle unfolded as Samuel proclaimed that because Saul had rejected the word of the Lord, God had rejected Saul as king. Samuel prophesied that Saul's kingdom would be torn away from him and given to another man. All eyes, especially Saul's, were upon Samuel as he left in disgust. Everyone knew that Samuel would go to seek the new king; they also knew that Saul would do anything to kill whomever Samuel chose. The elders of Bethlehem had good reason to be fearful; they did not want Saul and his army to bear down upon them in his attempt to destroy any potential successor.

Samuel said that he was there merely to offer a sacrifice for sin and to partake of a meal. Yet it seemed that the man of God was looking for something when he called for Jesse's sons. After the last of them stood before him, Samuel asked, "Are all your sons here?"

"There remains yet the youngest," replied Jesse.

"Send and get him, for we will not sit down till he comes," Samuel said. When David was brought to the prophet, Samuel took a flask of oil and anointed him in front of his brothers. No pronouncement was made, and few knew what had happened, but David experienced God's Spirit in a unique way from that moment forward. God was grooming David to become the next king of Israel.

David's Humble Beginning

One of the themes of the story of David is that God's call is not limited by heritage or circumstances. Unlike Abraham's privileged status as the firstborn, David was the youngest of eight brothers. Unlike the royal childhood of Moses, David was raised as a shepherd.

David was initially brought before King Saul because of his musical skills. Saul was tormented at night and could not sleep, and only David's skillful playing upon a lyre could soothe him. Music played such an important role in David's life that Scripture records a song that he wrote just before his death.[1] Most of the Psalms are attributed to David, whose heartfelt lyrics still connect with us and instruct us in our worship before God.

Even though David was initially known only as a skilled musician in Saul's court, he became famous when the neighboring Philistines declared war on Israel. Both armies filled opposite mountainsides with their troops, and the Philistines issued a challenge: If anyone could beat their champion, a huge warrior named Goliath, the Philistines would surrender to Israel and become their servants. If not, the Israelites would become slaves to the Philistines. The account of David and Goliath is famous as a story of the little guy beating the giant, but it was also a confirmation to the Israelites of a shift of power: They watched King Saul wither in fear before them as young David conquered overwhelming odds and killed Goliath with a simple slingshot. The shepherd boy had become a warrior.

Saul Attempts to Kill David

Saul's jealousy of David grew. Saul realized that he had lost touch with God's Spirit and was desperate for spiritual guidance. But Saul had trouble hearing God, while God seemed to guide David's every step. Saul realized that his grip on the throne was slipping and he could see only one solution: David must be killed.

Each attempt Saul made to kill David failed. David's continued military victories only caused the people to love him more. It seemed that David was unstoppable in all that he did. David had changed from a warrior to a great commander of armies.

Saul's attempts to kill David intensified until David was running from a team of assassins, barely escaping with his life. The great commander had become a fugitive, and for the next eight years David hid from Saul in caves and in the wilderness.

Outcast

There were many times when these circumstances overwhelmed David and he must have thought that he would never be king as God had promised. We can see this in Psalm 142, which is thought to have been written by David while he was hiding inside a cave from Saul and his army.

> I cry out loudly to GOD,
> loudly I plead with GOD for mercy.
> I spill out all my complaints before him,
> and spell out my troubles in detail:
>
> "As I sink in despair, my spirit ebbing away,
> you know how I'm feeling,
> Know the danger I'm in,
> the traps hidden in my path.
> Look right, look left—
> there's not a soul who cares what happens!
> I'm up against it, with no exit—
> bereft, left alone.
> I cry out, GOD, call out:
> 'You're my last chance, my only hope for life!'
> Oh listen, please listen;
> I've never been this low.

Rescue me from those who are hunting me down;
I'm no match for them.
Get me out of this dungeon
so I can thank you in public.
Your people will form a circle around me
and you'll bring me showers of blessing!"

Psalm 142:1–7 THE MESSAGE

There is a similar pattern in the stories of many people in the Bible. The pathways toward God's plans for our lives are often confusing to us. David's despair in a cave mirrors Sarah's laughter of disbelief in the desert and Moses' fear that he could not be God's spokesman with a speech impediment. The Bible depicts men and women who experienced God's calling, yet their sense of a divine purpose did not keep them from going through times of extreme discouragement. They often thought that they were not going to make it, that they had been passed over by God, that their circumstances were pulling them away from God's plans. The biblical story of David reminds us that God is faithful to His purposes, even when our surroundings seem to suggest that we have been forgotten.

David could have killed Saul numerous times during those eight years, but David chose to leave Saul's fate in the hands of God. David's faith in God could be why David is referred to in Scripture as a "man after God's own heart." David was determined to honor God, even if that meant that his life would be put in danger.

At one point, Saul got so close to David that David had to flee into the enemy territory of Gath to escape. He even pledged allegiance to the Philistine king so that he would allow David to live, and David was seen as a traitor to Israel. His actions were so offensive that he would never be allowed to return to Israel. He would be a servant to the Philistines for the rest of his life.

But God had different plans.

As the Philistines prepared for battle against Israel, the king of Gath wanted David to be his personal bodyguard. Yet the other Philistine kings did not trust David or the men who followed him. They demanded that David and his small army leave the battlefield.

This turn of events proved to be to David's advantage. Not only was David spared from having to fight his own people, but Saul was killed in the battle and the Jewish army retreated to Israel. Saul's death gave David a way back into Israel. The Philistines would see David's return to Israel as an act of opposition to Saul's throne, while David saw it as the opportunity to claim the kingdom that God had promised him.

The traitor now became a king.

Establishing the Kingdom

David left the Philistine town of Ziklag and moved to Hebron, a city in Judah, where he was anointed the king of Judah. At the same time, one of Saul's sons was established as the king of the other tribes of Israel. War between the two Jewish kingdoms followed, and David increased his power with each military victory.

He married more wives, who gave him more potential heirs to his throne, but David's polygamy would come at great cost in the future. David's firstborn, Amnon, raped his half sister and was murdered by her brother. David's third son, Absalom, died in battle trying to take his father's throne, and Adonijah, David's fourth son, tried to take the throne while David was on his deathbed. Adonijah would be killed later when he challenged the kingship of his half brother, Solomon. David's household became a tragic tale of murder and revenge.

Eventually the house of Saul fell, and after much blood was spilled in a civil war, David became king of a reunited Israel. He promptly began to expand the borders of Israel. The first target was the Canaanite city of Jerusalem. After taking the city, David renamed it the City of David and made Jerusalem the capital of Israel.

David also began a campaign of spiritual renewal so that the Israelites would return to God. He set up a tent in Jerusalem for worship and then placed the ark of God inside the tent. The ark was built by Moses to hold the tablets of the law and to be a place in which God displayed His presence. It was a point of blessing, or even a curse, if someone approached it carelessly and irreverently, yet David brought the ark into Jerusalem with dancing and music. He didn't care what others thought; David was a king who worshiped God with all of his heart.

David's Sin

Just like ours, David's life was filled with moments of achievement and moments of setback. As David experienced God's favor in all that he did, he decided to send his army into battle while he stayed behind in Jerusalem. It was during this time that he saw a beautiful woman named Bathsheba bathing on a nearby rooftop. David committed adultery with Bathsheba, and when she became pregnant, he had her husband killed in order to cover up what they had done.

David used his position as king to destroy a marriage and to kill a godly man. His abuse of power caused the prophet Nathan to expose David's sin and pronounce judgment on him and on Israel for his actions. But David realized that his sin was ultimately only against a holy God. In a psalm of lament over this shameful episode, David writes:

> Against you, you only, have I sinned
> and done what is evil in your sight,
> so that you are proved right when you speak
> and justified when you judge.
>
> Surely you desire truth in the inner parts;
> you teach me wisdom in the inmost place.
>
> Create in me a pure heart, O God,
> and renew a steadfast spirit within me.
> Do not cast me from your presence
> or take your Holy Spirit from me.
> Restore to me the joy of your salvation
> and grant me a willing spirit, to sustain me.
>   Psalm 51:4, 6, 10–12 NIV1984

David sinned under the law of Moses, but he also understood that only God's grace could uphold him. Instead of running away from God when he sinned, David ran toward Him. David understood something of the nature of God that would only be revealed much later through prophets like Jeremiah, and ultimately through Jesus: God wanted to heal the wounded heart from sin. In a sense, David was an Old Testament man with a New Testament understanding.

After David

The king was a man who received forgiveness for his sin. This would be dramatically displayed as David and Bathsheba had another son, named Solomon, who would eventually become heir to David's throne and one of the greatest leaders in the history of Israel. Solomon stood as a living testimony that God had redeemed David's greatest failure. Bathsheba was an adulteress; now she was the mother of the new king.

126

What ran through the mind of King David as he lay on his deathbed, listening to the thunderous sound of trumpeters, flutes, and people shouting in celebration of the new king of Israel? Would he have remembered his days as a shepherd? What thoughts did David have when he heard of Solomon's head being anointed with oil by the prophet?

The Bible allows us to see the entire life of David, from his adventures as a youth to his rise to power as a king, and eventually to his death. He was a man like us, battered and even warped by the trials of his life, yet upheld by the faithfulness of God. There were times when David was the general of an army, and other times when he pretended to be a lunatic to escape the sword of Saul. In the midst of this, David was primarily a man whose identity did not come from his circumstances but from God.

David's life took many twists and turns, but as he looked at his son Solomon taking the throne, David wanted him to know what would anchor him in the uncertainties of life:

> Keep the charge of the LORD your God, to walk in His ways, to keep His statutes, His commandments, His ordinances, and His testimonies, according to what is written in the Law of Moses, that you may succeed in all that you do and wherever you turn, so that the LORD may carry out His promise which He spoke concerning me, saying, "If your sons are careful of their way, to walk before Me in truth with all their heart and with all their soul, you shall not lack a man on the throne of Israel."
>
> 1 Kings 2:3–4 NASB

Our lives go in directions that we never planned for. We may even think that our mistakes have totally disqualified us from ever approaching God again. The life of David tells us something very different. God can work with and through all of the challenges we face externally and internally in our lives.

Yet the ultimate challenge that Solomon faced, as do all of us today, is that no matter how hard we try, we can't keep all of the statutes, commandments, ordinances, and testimonies of God. Solomon eventually worshiped the gods of his many wives and thus failed in his attempt to walk in God's truth with all of his heart and soul. As soon as Solomon died, the nation of Israel plunged into a civil war that divided the kingdom and made them easy prey for the Babylonian Empire, which became the next dominant force in the world.

God then set the stage for someone who would be able to fulfill everything that Moses had mandated. Coming from the lineage of David, this person would walk before God in truth and not falter. God was preparing the Jewish people for the true King who would inaugurate a kingdom that would fill the earth and know no end.

CHAPTER 11

The Prophetic Literature

If Christ is the climax of the story, the Old Testament sets the stage and begins the plot. Do you read just the endings of books?

Mark Dever

One of the questions I constantly get is, "If Christianity is so great, why is the church filled with hypocrites?" For some, the question is a desire to understand. For others, it represents a need to vent frustration to a person like me who, as a pastor, represents all they held dear in their earlier church upbringing.

I didn't see this job description in any ministerial handbook, yet it has become a very important role for me and for other pastors in recent years. People need an outlet for the anger they now feel from being hurt by the church. I have heard so many stories of clergy or church abuse that I have wondered at times if being in vocational ministry is such a good idea.

In this day of social networking and instant communication, we are painfully aware of the problems that have plagued the church lately. The stories of failed marriages among Christian leaders now make headline news. Prominent ministers who are accused of financial or moral improprieties attempt to outmaneuver their critics with sophisticated marketing instead of humility and vulnerability. Instead of fostering trust, these actions only breed greater suspicion about what goes on behind closed doors.

The suspicion that many people have about the church is legitimate—there *are* a lot of hypocrites in the church.

What may be surprising is that this problem is totally in line with what is recorded in the Bible.

One of the things that makes the Bible so unique compared to other religious works is that it has a built-in critique for religious abuse. The agents of that critique are called the prophets.

The term *prophet* can be conceived of in a number of ways. Some imagine a man dressed like John the Baptist, depicted in the book of Matthew—clothes of camel's hair, leather belt, and an unusual diet (from our perspective).[1] Some people think of figures such as Nostradamus, whom they claim had an ability to predict the future. All of us have heard of those who roam the streets warning people the end of the world is near.

Whereas some biblical prophets had the ability to see what was to come in the future, by and large, their main job was to call the people of God back to the ways of God. They had a unique ability to hear the voice of God coupled with an awareness that they were to proclaim what they heard to those around them. This makes the prophets an important part of God's story in the Scriptures.

The majority of the books in the Bible are prophetic books. It seems that people have been abusing the knowledge of God for misguided ends or personal gain for a long time. In fact, if we take a hard look at the history of the church, every doctrine in the Bible has been abused in one way or another.

This is exactly what the Bible teaches. The Bible talks explicitly about false prophets and their ability to turn people away from God,[2] so from the Bible's perspective, each generation has to be on guard against these enemies of God. We are expected to be able to test the prophets to see what is of God and what is not.[3]

The prophetic books of the Bible expose religious abuse and call us back to the words of God. In many ways, the answer to the abuses of religion is not to drift away from the Bible but to dig deeper.

More so than for most books of the Bible, to understand the prophets you need some knowledge of their circumstances. This is where study tools can help immensely. A Bible dictionary is invaluable for that. For more in-depth study, there are many commentaries of the individual books available. These can be extremely helpful in understanding references that the writer assumed everyone knew about, but which, thousands of years later, have become unclear. There are recommendations for more tools in appendix B.

Most of the prophetic books in the Old Testament were written in a 300-year window (Jonah in 770 BC to Malachi in 460 BC). During this time, a civil war split the Hebrew people into a Northern Kingdom (Israel) and a Southern Kingdom (Judah). Facing both internal strife and hostile foreign forces, the people of God needed to be reminded of the God who is faithful to His covenant even when they are not. The prophets became God's mouthpiece to His people to guide them through this very challenging period.

One example is in the book of Jeremiah. Jeremiah was a voice of correction to the abuses of the temple priests of his day. Listen to his prophetic lament in chapter 3:

"But like a woman unfaithful to her husband,
so you have been unfaithful to me, O house of Israel,"
declares the LORD.
A cry is heard on the barren heights,
the weeping and pleading of the people of Israel,
because they have perverted their ways
and have forgotten the LORD their God.
"Return, faithless people,
I will cure you of backsliding."
"Yes, we will come to you,
for you are the LORD our God."

Jeremiah 3:20–22 NIV 1984

According to Jeremiah, once God's people received a blessing, they turned to their own plans and ambitions, using religious offices and language but not wanting to follow after God. This theme is woven throughout the prophetic books, which are normally categorized as the Major and Minor Prophets.

Don't let the categories Major and Minor throw you off. This is only a reference to the size of their books. There is no distinction based upon how important they are to the identity of Israel or Judah in their day or to help us understand God's interactions with His people. Another thing to note is that the prophetic books are not arranged in chronological order in your Bible. This can be a little confusing as we go through a brief summary of the books of the prophets. As a result, I will also give a slight explanation of the background that each book addresses:

There are four Major Prophets in the Old Testament:

Isaiah—The most quoted prophet in the New Testament, Isaiah prepared the divided nations of Judah and Israel for the coming invasion by Assyria. There are so many prophecies about Jesus Christ in this book that Augustine called it "the fifth gospel."

Isaiah gives us insight into the fall of a nation and the faithfulness of God in the midst of that decline.

Jeremiah—Known as the weeping prophet, Jeremiah spoke to Judah after Assyria had lost its power and Babylon had destroyed the temple. Jeremiah is a reference point for people who feel crushed in the midst of very disturbing circumstances. He is also credited with writing the book of Lamentations.

Ezekiel—Ezekiel was exiled to Babylon with many other Jewish leaders after the destruction of the temple. Prophesying after Jeremiah, Ezekiel gives us visions of God's holiness and glory as he spoke to a people who were under the weight of judgment. Yet even this would not stop God in His purposes—He would breathe new life into a people who were dead in their sins.

Daniel—Another exile in Babylon, Daniel stands as a witness that it is possible to live a fruitful life in the midst of a culture that is hostile to all that you believe. Daniel proclaims God's sovereignty to Babylon at the height of its power and arrogance. In the fulfillment of Daniel's predictions, Daniel watched Babylon fall under Persian rule.

There are also twelve Minor Prophets in the Old Testament:

Hosea—Written prior to Isaiah, in this book God tells Hosea to marry a prostitute in order to confront Northern Israel with its unfaithfulness to God. Through this unusual action, God also dramatically declares His love and desire for His people. Hosea proclaims a God who is not distant and detached, but passionate for His people.

Joel—There is some debate about when this book was written, but many scholars place it after the exile to Babylon. Hordes of locusts have destroyed the crops of Israel, and Joel calls the locusts the "army of the Lord," sent to humble God's people and bring them back to himself. This book emphasizes the day of the Lord, when His judgment will come to all the earth.

Amos—Probably written around the time of Hosea, Amos prophesied during a period when Assyria was ebbing in power and both Israel and Judah were prospering. But this was not to be a sign of God's blessing, for Amos correctly foretold the resurgence of Assyria. Israel saw a "golden age," but Amos had the hard task of telling them that they were about to be overrun again.

Obadiah—Even though the Edomites were descendants of Jacob's brother Esau, they took advantage of Jerusalem when it fell to Babylon. Obadiah proclaims a judgment upon Edom for their treachery. This book ends with the promise that God's kingdom will prevail.

Jonah—Known for being in the belly of a fish for three days, Jonah has profound implications because the heathen in the account are more compassionate and quick to repent than the prophet. Jonah tells us how God has always had a plan to reach all nations for His glory.

Micah—Listing a large number of sins, Micah tells Israel that Babylon and Assyria will be God's instruments of judgment against them. Yet in the midst of this, Micah speaks of a Shepherd King who will gather and lead a remnant forward.

Nahum—Nahum prophesied the destruction of Nineveh at the height of its power, and it fell just sixty years later. Nahum reminds us that God is still in charge, even when His people are not. There is nothing that God cannot use for His purposes, and there is no nation that can intimidate God.

Habakkuk—Written as a dialogue with God, Habakkuk complains about the moral decay of Israel. It is in this environment that Habakkuk tells us that "the righteous shall live by faith," which becomes a major theme of the apostle Paul's writings in the New Testament.

Zephaniah—In spite of having seen the destruction and exile of Israel a generation or two previous, Judah refuses to turn back as a nation to its covenant obligations to God. Zephaniah reminds Judah that there is no such thing as a second-generation child of God. Every generation must own God's covenant, not relying on the faith of a previous generation.

Haggai—Haggai prophesied to the people of Jerusalem after they had returned from Babylon but before they rebuilt the temple. The city of Jerusalem lay in ruins, the walls and the temple having been destroyed by the Babylonians. Haggai, together with Zechariah, called upon the people to stop focusing on their own economic well-being, and to complete the temple.

Zechariah—Written around the same time as Haggai, the Jews had returned from being exiled in Babylon, but they were discouraged by the slow progress of rebuilding their national identity. Zechariah reminded God's people that returning to their homeland would do them no good if in their hearts they did not return to God.

Malachi—The final book in the Old Testament, Malachi deals with Israel at a time when they had reestablished the temple yet had not become a world power. Malachi strongly rebukes the apathy of his time, but this book ends with a promise for the return of Elijah to restore the hearts of families. Four hundred years of silence follows this book until John the Baptist appears in the gospel accounts.

The Bible is also filled with prophets who never wrote their own book. Men like Elijah[4] and Elisha[5] played pivotal roles in the identity of the Israelites as God's chosen people. Miriam[6] and Deborah[7] are identified as women prophets, or prophetesses. The New Testament described a prophet named Agabus,[8] who told Paul about the imprisonment that awaited him on his journey. These books were not just meant to record ancient Jewish history. The apostle Peter helps us understand some of the implications of reading the prophets of old today.

The prophets who prophesied of the grace that was to be yours searched and inquired about this salvation, they inquired what person or time was indicated by the Spirit of Christ within them when predicting the sufferings of Christ and the subsequent glory. It was revealed to them that they were serving not themselves but you, in the things which have now been announced to you by those who preached the good news to you through the Holy Spirit sent from heaven, things into which angels long to look.

1 Peter 1:10–12 RSV

So when the people of Israel had returned from their exile in Babylon and were struggling to rebuild their temple, Zechariah writes:

Rejoice, O people of Zion!
Shout in triumph, O people of Jerusalem!
Look, your king is coming to you.
He is righteous and victorious,
yet he is humble, riding on a donkey—
riding on a donkey's colt.

Zechariah 9:9 NLT

The prophet was telling the people that their efforts to rebuild Jerusalem were not in vain, but we can also see how Matthew and John would use this unapologetically when they described Jesus Christ coming into Jerusalem.[9] The prophets were pointing not only to their day, but to a day yet to come—and that day was fulfilled in Christ.

Revelation

The New Testament contains what many consider to be the most challenging prophetic book of all to understand, much less to apply. Filled with images of dragons, angels, flying cities, and much more, John's Revelation poses so many problems in understanding its meaning that it is either ignored or sensationalized.

It stands out from the other prophetic books in a number of ways. Instead of a narrative, the book of Revelation is a specific form of literature, called "apocalyptic literature." It is not based upon real events, but on visions or dreams. The imagery that is used was tied to specific references in John's day; many of these images are clear, but some we can only speculate about. This puts all of us at a disadvantage in understanding the meaning of beasts coming out of the sea with many heads or who the great whore of Babylon is. This has also made the book of Revelation vulnerable to misuse by preachers who take advantage of the book's vagueness for their own interpretations and agendas.

But even if you don't get much out of Revelation, there is a reward promised for the effort of reading it:

> Blessed is he that readeth, and they that hear the words of this prophecy, and keep those things which are written therein: for the time is at hand.
>
> Revelation 1:3 KJV

The prophets give us a tremendous insight about how easy it is to fall into apathy toward the things of God. When we expose ourselves to their writings, we become more aware of the hypocrisies that can creep into our souls and our communities. The prophets also remind us of God's faithfulness to His people, even if those reminders are harsh, abrasive, and even hard to understand. The prophets exposed the need for a Savior, One who would deliver God's people from their sins once and for all.

Summary

The prophets are a vital part of God's ecosystem. Just as they challenged the hypocrisy of the people of Israel, they challenge us when we have strayed and call us back to God's heart. The historical background the prophets faced can unlock valuable insights into the real issues they had to confront, and can help us confront our own issues today.

CHAPTER 12

Jesus: God With Us

The Kingdom of God Is at Hand

> The time is fulfilled, and the kingdom of God is at hand. Repent, and believe in the gospel.
>
> Mark 1:15 NKJV

Jesus' first words in Mark's gospel commanded the attention of those around Him. The time is fulfilled: The story that has been progressively unfolding in Israel has reached its climax. The kingdom of God is at hand: From this point on things will change. Repent, and believe in the gospel: The good news that is coming to you will demand that you change the way you are living.

His audience probably heard this with mixed emotions. The Jewish people had been ruled by the Roman Empire for more than forty years. To them, the coming of God's kingdom would mean the end of Roman rule, the restoration of Israel as a sovereign nation, and the fulfillment of many prophecies that they had read about all of their lives.

But the Roman Empire seemed invincible. Other leaders had tried to overthrow the Romans, saying that they were bringing God's new kingdom, and they had miserably failed. What kind of good news could Jesus have that would cause the kind of change the Jews expected? What would set Him apart from the others?

Yet Jesus wasn't like the other religious teachers. There was an authority to His voice that caused people to leave all that they had to follow Him. He quickly gained a group of followers, or disciples, and taught them to see the law of Moses in an entirely new way. The gospel of Matthew records that it wasn't long before crowds started following Jesus as He preached the good news of the kingdom throughout Galilee.[1]

What was the good news of the kingdom of God? Luke records a time when Jesus entered a synagogue to give a customary Scripture reading. He opened a scroll that contained the writings of Isaiah and read aloud:

> "The Spirit of the Lord is on me,
> because he has anointed me
> to preach good news to the poor.
> He has sent me to proclaim freedom for the prisoners
> and recovery of sight for the blind,
> to release the oppressed,
> to proclaim the year of the Lord's favor."
>
> Then he rolled up the scroll, gave it back to the attendant and sat down. The eyes of everyone in the synagogue were fastened on him, and he began by saying to them, "Today this scripture is fulfilled in your hearing."
>
> Luke 4:18–21 NIV1984

This was a kingdom that belonged to the poor and the disempowered, the sick and the outcasts. This kingdom was different from the elite religious hierarchies that had been set up in collaboration with the Roman rulers, in which the rich and powerful were supposed to be the ones accepted and blessed by God. Yet Jesus showed that the kingdom He preached about was found throughout Scripture. The Law and the Prophets had been pointing to this moment all along.

Jesus had plenty of skeptics. They argued with Him about His views on the Jewish Scriptures, but they could say little about the miracles He performed everywhere He went. How could they deny His teachings when His miracles were directly linked to what He said?

Virgin Birth

Jesus' miracles challenge us as well. The first miracle was His birth. The Bible states that Jesus Christ was born of a young virgin named Mary. Mary claimed to have been impregnated by the Holy Spirit. Her fiancé, Joseph, would have broken off the engagement, but he had a dream in which God told him to marry her.

At Jesus' birth, wise men arrived from a far country bringing gifts, and angels appeared to shepherds proclaiming that the Savior of the earth had been born. This first miracle alone is enough to make sensible people wonder if what they are reading is history or myth.

Yet the virgin birth is important in understanding the rest of Jesus' life. Jesus claimed that He and His heavenly Father were one. At one point, He made an outrageous statement:

"Abraham—your 'father'—with jubilant faith looked down the corridors of history and saw my day coming. He saw it and cheered."

The Jews said, "You're not even fifty years old—and Abraham saw you?"

141

"Believe me," said Jesus, "*I am who I am* long before Abraham was anything."

That did it—pushed them over the edge. They picked up rocks to throw at him. But Jesus slipped away, getting out of the Temple.

John 8:56–59 THE MESSAGE

Why did they try to kill Jesus? He used the same name that God used for himself when He spoke to Moses at the burning bush. Jesus said that He was that same God.

So there is a heavenly logic to the virgin birth. That God was His father pointed to Jesus's divinity, that a woman was His mother pointed to Jesus' humanity. This is what caused the apostle Paul to call Jesus the second Adam[2]; both have only God as their natural Father. If it had been different, we should be skeptical of all Jesus' claims about himself.

The virgin birth immediately challenges our belief—and this is the point, for the birth of Jesus Christ sets the tone for the rest of the story. If we don't marvel at the birth story, how can we accept the miracles that followed? From His birth to His resurrection, Jesus' life is one of supernatural wonder.

Water Into Wine

Jesus began His ministry as a rabbi when He was thirty years old. The first miracle recorded in John's gospel occurred at a wedding feast. Jesus, His mother, and His disciples heard that the groom had run out of wine. In that culture, running out of wine at a wedding would have been a major embarrassment for the family. Jesus told the groom's servants to bring six large jars and fill them with water. As the servants filled the jars to the brim, they realized that the water had turned into wine.

This miracle had great significance: Unlike how many of us

picture God, as somber or condemning, Jesus first revealed the power of God during a celebration. Jesus did not emphasize a set of rules, but festival joy. This miracle was also the forerunner of another wedding feast. At the end of the book of Revelation, the Lord sets a table for the bride of Christ and His Son. The wine that we have today is nothing compared to the wine that He will serve at that event. The first miracle of Jesus invites us to taste and see that He is good.

Forgiven

Jesus always emphasized God's goodness. He healed people and delivered them from spiritual oppression because He was not as interested in obedience to religious rules as He was in their love. This message was not well received by the religious leaders in Jerusalem, but it was embraced as wonderful news by the rest of the people.

One of the clearest instances of this occurred while Jesus was at a religious leader's house for a meal. A woman with a bad reputation (she could have been a prostitute) heard that Jesus was there and got into the house. Once she saw Him, she knelt at His feet weeping, then wiped her tears from His feet with her hair. At that time, women kept their heads covered, so the exposure of her hair would imply either her sensuality or her ignorance of religious practices. She then took costly perfume and began to anoint Jesus' feet.

This caused the religious leader of the house to question how "special" Jesus was:

> "If this man were a prophet, he would have known who and what sort of woman this is who is touching him, for she is a sinner."
>
> And Jesus answering said to him, "Simon, I have something to say to you." And he answered, "Say it, Teacher."

"A certain moneylender had two debtors. One owed five hundred denarii, and the other fifty. When they could not pay, he cancelled the debt of both. Now which of them will love him more?" Simon answered, "The one, I suppose, for whom he cancelled the larger debt." And he said to him, "You have judged rightly." Then turning toward the woman he said to Simon, "Do you see this woman? I entered your house; you gave me no water for my feet, but she has wet my feet with her tears and wiped them with her hair. You gave me no kiss, but from the time I came in she has not ceased to kiss my feet. You did not anoint my head with oil, but she has anointed my feet with ointment. Therefore I tell you, her sins, which are many, are forgiven—for she loved much. But he who is forgiven little, loves little." And he said to her, "Your sins are forgiven." Then those who were at table with him began to say among themselves, "Who is this, who even forgives sins?" And he said to the woman, "Your faith has saved you; go in peace."

Luke 7:39–50

Proclaiming forgiveness for this woman was something that only priests could do, and even then it would have to be accompanied with a sacrifice for sin. Jesus' actions were offensive to the religious community, but for the woman, it was an act of grace. When Jesus proclaimed a similar forgiveness of sins over a paralytic in a bed, the religious leaders fumed to each other, "Why does this man speak like that? He is blaspheming! Who can forgive sins but God alone?"[3]

Lord Save Us

The crowds who followed Jesus grew as the stories of His miracles spread throughout the region. It must have looked like a small army following Him. Jesus was in His third year of ministry. It would have been the perfect time for Him to make His move to become a political leader of the kingdom that He had been talking about. He did something radically different instead:

> And as Jesus was about to go up to Jerusalem, He took the twelve disciples aside by themselves, and on the way He said to them, "Behold, we are going up to Jerusalem, and the Son of Man will be delivered to the chief priests and scribes, and they will condemn Him to death, and will hand Him over to the Gentiles to mock and scourge and crucify Him, and on the third day He will be raised up."
>
> Matthew 20:17–19 NASB

Instead of continuing to build a following large enough to overthrow the Roman authorities, Jesus decided to go straight to the seat of Roman and Jewish power at that time: Jerusalem.

Going to Jerusalem meant that Jesus could be captured or even killed. His disciples couldn't understand His thinking. Peter, the most vocal of Jesus' disciples, even tried to talk Jesus out of it, but Jesus knew what God His Father wanted. Like Abraham prepared to offer his son as a sacrifice, Jesus was prepared to go to the place of His sacrifice.

As Jesus entered Jerusalem, throngs of people waved palm branches and shouted *"Hosanna!"* which means, "Lord, save us!" They were excited about having a new king of Israel. They expected Him to take over the city. But when He reached Jerusalem, Jesus found a private room where He could have a meal with His disciples, which we now call the Last Supper. Jesus broke a loaf of bread and passed the pieces to His disciples, saying that the bread symbolized His body that was about to be broken. Then He served them wine, saying that it stood for His blood that was about to be shed for the forgiveness of their sins. After that, one of Jesus' disciples, Judas, left in order to betray Jesus to the Roman authorities.

Condemned

Roman soldiers arrived at night and arrested Jesus. His disciples scattered in all directions to save their lives. The Roman governor, Pilate, determined that Jesus had not broken any Roman laws, but the priests incited the crowds against Him. Though Pilate tried to release Jesus, the crowds continually demanded that Jesus be killed for claiming to be the Son of God.

Pilate realized that if he didn't condemn Jesus to death, he could face a riot from the Jews. He sentenced Jesus to die by being nailed to a cross.

Jesus' death was slow and agonizing. Roman soldiers whipped Him, then made a crown of thorns and pressed it into His head, mocking Him as the "King of the Jews." Beaten again, Jesus carried His own cross until He could bear it no more and it was laid on the shoulders of Simon from Cyrene, who carried it to the top of the hill, where they nailed Jesus' hands and feet to the wooden beams and hoisted Him up.

The crowds taunted Jesus while His mother and a few friends watched helplessly. "He saved others, why can't He save himself?" they said. "Come down from the cross if you are the Son of God." Then something unusual happened. Darkness covered the land for three hours, beginning at noon. At three in the afternoon, Jesus cried out, "My God, my God, why have you forsaken me?" The teacher who had said that God knows every hair on our heads experienced separation from His Father for the first time. After this, Jesus said, "It is finished," and took His last breath. It was the time of the evening sacrifice in the temple.

Breaking the legs of a crucified man was a merciful way to speed the victim's death, but Jesus was already dead by the time the soldiers approached him. To confirm his death, a soldier pierced Jesus' side with a spear. Water and blood came out—the threat from the "King of the Jews" was over. The hope of a new kingdom seemed finished.

Resurrection

The Jewish leaders were concerned about rumors that Jesus would rise from the dead or that His disciples would steal His body and claim that He had risen, so they set a guard in front of the tomb. They also rolled a large stone over the tomb's opening. They wanted the Christian movement to end.

Mary Magdalene and Jesus' mother, Mary, came to the tomb on the third day and witnessed a spectacular event. The Roman guards thought there was an earthquake, but Matthew records that an angel came down from heaven and removed the stone. The guards were petrified with fear while the angel of the Lord explained to the women what had happened:

> Do not be afraid, for I know that you are looking for Jesus, who was crucified. He is not here; he has risen, just as he said. Come and see the place where he lay. Then go quickly and tell his disciples: "He has risen from the dead and is going ahead of you into Galilee. There you will see him." Now I have told you.
>
> 28:5–7 NIV1984

The first people to carry the good news of the risen Christ were women, which was radically countercultural in a society where women were not even considered legitimate witnesses in court.

The resurrected Jesus appeared many times to His followers, yet many of them doubted. Just like in the days of Moses, even great displays of power were not enough to convince hearts that were determined to believe only what they could fully understand. Like His birth and life, the death and resurrection of Jesus defies rational explanation. The only way that Jesus' disciples (and we today) could accept this was to surrender to the fact that with God, all things are possible.

Jesus' resurrection (and the subsequent outpouring of the Holy Spirit, recorded in the book of Acts) was the sign that God the Father had accepted the death of Jesus as the ultimate sacrifice for our sins. The resurrection showed that a new kingdom truly had come—though it was not the kingdom the Jews had expected. It was a kingdom that would go beyond Israel to the far reaches of the earth, and it has not diminished since that day.

Epilogue

A Final Word

In the beginning was the Word, and the Word was with God, and
the Word was God. He was with God in the beginning.

John 1:1–2 NIV 1984

John begins his gospel of Jesus with this epic statement,
connecting us to the first words of Genesis. As the Spirit
of the Lord hovered over the deep, Genesis records that God
said, "Let there be light."[1] Creation began with a word, and
in some mysterious way, John tells us that Jesus was with God
at the beginning. This language leads us to the doctrine of the
Trinity, which says that God is three persons, yet one being.[2]
Though the word *Trinity* is not in the Bible, the concept is there
from Genesis to Revelation.

An awareness of the Trinity is very important in reading the
Bible, for the God of the Old Testament is also the God of the
New Testament. This is what caused the New Testament writers

to see the Old Testament as a treasure chest of information about the fulfillment of all things in Jesus Christ.[3] The flame that was seen over the heads of the disciples in the upper room[4] is directly linked to the fire that confronted Moses in the burning bush.[5]

That should be enough to baffle any of us, but John doesn't stop there:

> And the Word became flesh, and dwelt among us, and we saw His glory, glory as of the only begotten from the Father, full of grace and truth.
>
> John 1:14 NASB

The Word dwelt among us. The original Greek makes the point even more dramatically: He "pitched his tent among us." This is a direct reference to the tent of Moses, where God dwelt among His people. John tells us that the new dwelling place of God is in Jesus Christ, who came to earth to bring grace and truth together. God's truth (His absolute holiness) met with grace (His unmerited favor) in Jesus.

The God of creation is not aloof and inaccessible in heaven— He has become one of us. When Jesus came to earth, John saw His glory—a glory so encompassing that it changed everything John thought about the world around him. This is more than just something that is written, it is a new way to see everything that we know.

What if the Bible was created to change the way we see things? Jesus promised that the Holy Spirit would "guide us into all truth."[6] As we approach the Scriptures with a desire to know God, we are not reading alone, relying on our own ability to comprehend. The Holy Spirit helps us.

But when we approach the Bible this way, new ways of seeing things present us with an alarming thought. According to Scripture, the rebellion of Adam and Eve caused all of us to be plagued by sin. Even our perceptions of God are distorted.[7] If we get anything from the story of God in the Scriptures, it is that He is forever holy and we are continually rebelling against Him and His ways. We are hopelessly lost without the intervention of God. We need help. The reality of our situation is that we need grace.

That is why Jesus came to earth. Since God is holy and cannot allow sin to be in His presence, Adam's sin separated all of us from God. But because this holy God loves His children, He intervened. He came and dwelt among us. Since we couldn't keep His commandments, God himself kept them as a man. He lived the life that we were supposed to live and died on the cross as a blameless, innocent man—the only completely innocent man who ever lived.

At the cross, grace and truth met each other in such a profound way that the earth became dark, the ground shook, and the curtain in the temple separating God's presence from us was torn from the top down.[8] The judgment of a holy God upon rebellious humanity was finally satisfied at the cross.

It is interesting that the first thing to occur after this phenomenon was understanding: A Roman centurion and those with him said, "Truly this was the Son of God." The people who nailed Jesus to the cross were some of the first to acknowledge who Jesus was.

God intervened at the cross of Jesus Christ, and with the same power that raised Jesus from the dead three days later, He has been opening hearts ever since.

One of those hearts belonged to Blaise Pascal. By the time Pascal died in 1662, at the age of thirty-nine, his achievements had changed the world. Pascal published his first notable work on geometry at the age of sixteen. At nineteen, he invented a calculating machine that many historians consider one of the world's first computers.

Pascal's conversion to Christianity was also well known. His letters and theological work are considered masterpieces of French writing. Pascal was a philosopher, a great writer, an innovator in mathematics, and a theologian.

After his death, a servant found an object sewn inside Pascal's jacket. It was a hidden document that gives us insight into the motivation of this great mind. Here is an excerpt:

> The year of grace 1654, Monday, 23 November. From about half-past ten in the evening until about half-past twelve, midnight, FIRE. God of Abraham, God of Isaac, God of Jacob, not of the philosophers nor of the Wise. Assurance, joy, assurance, feeling, joy, peace. Just Father, the world has not known thee but I have known thee. Joy, joy, joy, tears of joy. I do not separate myself from thee. This is eternal life that they should know thee the only true God and him whom thou hast sent. JESUS CHRIST—JESUS CHRIST. I shall not forget what you have taught me. Amen.

What Pascal encountered was more than a philosophy. He had experienced something that he defined as supernatural. God's intervention in Blaise Pascal's life caused him to seek the Scriptures to try to explain what had happened to him. He saw the world in a new way.

Maybe what has happened in your life is not as dramatic as what happened to Pascal, but the fact that you are reading this book is a sign of a burning desire to know God. God has put that fire in you. Your job is to fan the flame.

The goal in reading the Bible is not to merely read the Bible. The goal of reading the Bible is to get to know and interact with the God of the Bible. As Paul told his young disciple, Timothy:

> All Scripture is breathed out by God and profitable for teaching, for reproof, for correction, and for training in righteousness,

that the man of God may be competent, equipped for every good work.

2 Timothy 3:16–17

When Paul used the phrase *breathed out by God*, he, like John, was referring to the Genesis account, when God breathed His life into the dust and Adam came alive. That same breath is in the Scripture. God breathes life into us through His Word, and we can experience His care for us through it.

This is what transformed John and everyone else who has seen God's glory. In a wonderful and mysterious way, the Word has become flesh and dwells among us through the Holy Spirit. The barrier between God and man is gone; therefore the Scriptures come alive to us and speak to our soul.

The Law and the Prophets, the poetry, the letters of Paul, and the gospel accounts all point to the life, death, and resurrection of Jesus Christ. Jesus is God's ultimate word to humanity. As we read the Bible with anticipation, God will breathe His life into us as well.

Where there is breath, there is life. Where there is life, there is hope.

To the God of all hope.

Appendix A

A One-Year Bible-Reading Plan

Reading through the Bible in a year is a great way to get the big picture and allow the Holy Spirit to use the Scriptures to open your heart. I have chosen a chronological approach because you can then understand how the books of the Bible work together. For example, Job is placed after Genesis 11 because that is probably the era that Job describes, though most scholars agree that Job was written at a much later period. The Psalms are linked to the events and writers that inspired them.

I pray that this format of reading the Bible in a year will expand both your understanding of the Scriptures and how to apply that understanding toward your daily life.

☐ Jan. 1 Gen. 1–3	☐ Jan. 7 Job 14–16	☐ Jan. 13 Job 35–37
☐ Jan. 2 Gen. 4–7	☐ Jan. 8 Job 17–20	☐ Jan. 14 Job 38–39
☐ Jan. 3 Gen. 8–11	☐ Jan. 9 Job 21–23	☐ Jan. 15 Job 40–42
☐ Jan. 4 Job 1–5	☐ Jan. 10 Job 24–28	☐ Jan. 16 Gen. 12–15
☐ Jan. 5 Job 6–9	☐ Jan. 11 Job 29–31	☐ Jan. 17 Gen. 16–18
☐ Jan. 6 Job 10–13	☐ Jan. 12 Job 32–34	☐ Jan. 18 Gen. 19–21

☐ **Jan. 19** Gen. 22–24
☐ **Jan. 20** Gen. 25–26
☐ **Jan. 21** Gen. 27–29
☐ **Jan. 22** Gen. 30–31
☐ **Jan. 23** Gen. 32–34
☐ **Jan. 24** Gen. 35–37
☐ **Jan. 25** Gen. 38–40
☐ **Jan. 26** Gen. 41–42
☐ **Jan. 27** Gen. 43–45
☐ **Jan. 28** Gen. 46–47
☐ **Jan. 29** Gen. 48–50
☐ **Jan. 30** Ex. 1–3
☐ **Jan. 31** Ex. 4–6

☐ **Feb. 1** Ex. 7–9
☐ **Feb. 2** Ex. 10–12
☐ **Feb. 3** Ex. 13–15
☐ **Feb. 4** Ex. 16–18
☐ **Feb. 5** Ex. 19–21
☐ **Feb. 6** Ex. 22–24
☐ **Feb. 7** Ex. 25–27
☐ **Feb. 8** Ex. 28–29
☐ **Feb. 9** Ex. 30–32
☐ **Feb. 10** Ex. 33–35
☐ **Feb. 11** Ex. 36–38
☐ **Feb. 12** Ex. 39–40
☐ **Feb. 13** Lev. 1–4
☐ **Feb. 14** Lev. 5–7
☐ **Feb. 15** Lev. 8–10
☐ **Feb. 16** Lev. 11–13
☐ **Feb. 17** Lev. 14–15
☐ **Feb. 18** Lev. 16–18
☐ **Feb. 19** Lev. 19–21
☐ **Feb. 20** Lev. 22–23
☐ **Feb. 21** Lev. 24–25
☐ **Feb. 22** Lev. 26–27
☐ **Feb. 23** Num. 1–2
☐ **Feb. 24** Num. 3–4
☐ **Feb. 25** Num. 5–6
☐ **Feb. 26** Num. 7
☐ **Feb. 27** Num. 8–10
☐ **Feb. 28** Num. 11–13

☐ **Mar. 1** Num. 14–15;
Ps. 90
☐ **Mar. 2** Num. 16–17
☐ **Mar. 3** Num. 18–20

☐ **Mar. 4** Num. 21–22
☐ **Mar. 5** Num. 23–25
☐ **Mar. 6** Num. 26–27
☐ **Mar. 7** Num. 28–30
☐ **Mar. 8** Num. 31–32
☐ **Mar. 9** Num. 33–34
☐ **Mar. 10** Num. 35–36
☐ **Mar. 11** Deut. 1–2
☐ **Mar. 12** Deut. 3–4
☐ **Mar. 13** Deut. 5–7
☐ **Mar. 14** Deut. 8–10
☐ **Mar. 15** Deut. 11–13
☐ **Mar. 16** Deut. 14–16
☐ **Mar. 17** Deut. 17–20
☐ **Mar. 18** Deut. 21–23
☐ **Mar. 19** Deut. 24–27
☐ **Mar. 20** Deut. 28–29
☐ **Mar. 21** Deut. 30–31
☐ **Mar. 22** Deut. 32–34;
Ps. 91
☐ **Mar. 23** Josh. 1–4
☐ **Mar. 24** Josh. 5–8
☐ **Mar. 25** Josh. 9–11
☐ **Mar. 26** Josh. 12–15
☐ **Mar. 27** Josh. 16–18
☐ **Mar. 28** Josh. 19–21
☐ **Mar. 29** Josh. 22–24
☐ **Mar. 30** Judg. 1–2
☐ **Mar. 31** Judg. 3–5

☐ **Apr. 1** Judg. 6–7
☐ **Apr. 2** Judg. 8–9
☐ **Apr. 3** Judg. 10–12
☐ **Apr. 4** Judg. 13–15
☐ **Apr. 5** Judg. 16–18
☐ **Apr. 6** Judg. 19–21
☐ **Apr. 7** Ruth 1–4
☐ **Apr. 8** 1 Sam. 1–3
☐ **Apr. 9** 1 Sam. 4–8
☐ **Apr. 10** 1 Sam. 9–12
☐ **Apr. 11** 1 Sam. 13–14
☐ **Apr. 12** 1 Sam. 15–17
☐ **Apr. 13** 1 Sam. 18–20;
Ps. 11; Ps. 59
☐ **Apr. 14** 1 Sam. 21–24
☐ **Apr. 15** Ps. 7; Ps. 27;
Ps. 31; Ps. 34; Ps. 52

☐ **Apr. 16** Ps. 56; Ps. 120;
Ps. 140–142
☐ **Apr. 17** 1 Sam. 25–27
☐ **Apr. 18** Ps. 17; Ps. 35;
Ps. 54; Ps. 63
☐ **Apr. 19** 1 Sam. 28–31;
Ps. 18
☐ **Apr. 20** Ps. 121; Ps.
123–125; Ps. 128–130
☐ **Apr. 21** 2 Sam. 1–4
☐ **Apr. 22** Ps. 6; Ps. 8–10;
Ps. 14; Ps. 16; Ps. 19;
Ps. 21
☐ **Apr. 23** 1 Chron. 1–2
☐ **Apr. 24** Ps. 43–45; Ps.
49; Ps. 84–85; Ps. 87
☐ **Apr. 25** 1 Chron. 3–5
☐ **Apr. 26** Ps. 73; Ps.
77–78
☐ **Apr. 27** 1 Chron. 6
☐ **Apr. 28** Ps. 81; Ps. 88;
Ps. 92–93
☐ **Apr. 29** 1 Chron. 7–10
☐ **Apr. 30** Ps. 102–104

☐ **May 1** 2 Sam. 5:1–10;
1 Chron. 11–12
☐ **May 2** Ps. 133
☐ **May 3** Ps. 106–107
☐ **May 4** 2 Sam. 5:11–
6:23; 1 Chron. 13–16
☐ **May 5** Ps. 1–2; Ps.
15; Ps. 22–24, Ps. 47,
Ps. 68
☐ **May 6** Ps. 89, Ps. 96,
Ps. 100; Ps. 101; Ps.
105; Ps. 132
☐ **May 7** 2 Sam. 7;
1 Chron. 17
☐ **May 8** Ps. 25; Ps. 29;
Ps. 33; Ps. 36; Ps. 39
☐ **May 9** 2 Sam. 8–9;
1 Chron. 18
☐ **May 10** Ps. 50; Ps. 53;
Ps. 60; Ps. 75
☐ **May 11** 2 Sam. 10;
1 Chron. 19; Ps. 20

☐ **May 12** Ps. 65–67; Ps. 69–70

☐ **May 13** 2 Sam. 11–12; 1 Chron. 20

☐ **May 14** Ps. 32; Ps. 51; Ps. 86; Ps. 122

☐ **May 15** 2 Sam. 13–15

☐ **May 16** Ps. 3–4; Ps. 12–13; Ps. 28; Ps. 55

☐ **May 17** 2 Sam. 16–18

☐ **May 18** Ps. 26, Ps. 40, Ps. 58; Ps. 61–62; Ps. 64

☐ **May 19** 2 Sam. 19–21

☐ **May 20** Ps. 5; Ps. 38; Ps. 41–42

☐ **May 21** 2 Sam. 22–23; Ps. 57

☐ **May 22** Ps. 95; Ps. 97–99

☐ **May 23** 2 Sam. 24; 1 Chron. 21–22; Ps. 30

☐ **May 24** Ps. 108–110

☐ **May 25** 1 Chron. 23–25

☐ **May 26** Ps. 131; Ps. 138–139; Ps. 143–145

☐ **May 27** 1 Chron. 26–29; Ps. 127

☐ **May 28** Ps. 111–118

☐ **May 29** 1 Kings 1–2; Ps. 37; Ps. 71; Ps. 94

☐ **May 30** Ps. 119:1–88

☐ **May 31** 1 Kings 3–4; 2 Chron. 1; Ps. 72

☐ **Jun. 1** Ps. 119:89–176

☐ **Jun. 2** Song 1–8

☐ **Jun. 3** Prov. 1–3

☐ **Jun. 4** Prov. 4–6

☐ **Jun. 5** Prov. 7–9

☐ **Jun. 6** Prov. 10–12

☐ **Jun. 7** Prov. 13–15

☐ **Jun. 8** Prov. 16–18

☐ **Jun. 9** Prov. 19–21

☐ **Jun. 10** Prov. 22–24

☐ **Jun. 11** 1 Kings 5–6; 2 Chron. 2–3

☐ **Jun. 12** 1 Kings 7; 2 Chron. 4

☐ **Jun. 13** 1 Kings 8; 2 Chron. 5

☐ **Jun. 14** 2 Chron. 6–7; Ps. 136

☐ **Jun. 15** Ps. 134; Ps. 146–150

☐ **Jun. 16** 1 Kings 9; 2 Chron. 8

☐ **Jun. 17** Prov. 25–26

☐ **Jun. 18** Prov. 27–29

☐ **Jun. 19** Eccl. 1–6

☐ **Jun. 20** Eccl. 7–12

☐ **Jun. 21** 1 Kings 10–11; 2 Chron. 9

☐ **Jun. 22** Prov. 30–31

☐ **Jun. 23** 1 Kings 12–14

☐ **Jun. 24** 2 Chron. 10–12

☐ **Jun. 25** 1 Kings 15:1–24; 2 Chron. 13–16

☐ **Jun. 26** 1 Kings 15:25–16:34; 2 Chron. 17

☐ **Jun. 27** 1 Kings 17–19

☐ **Jun. 28** 1 Kings 20–21

☐ **Jun. 29** 1 Kings 22; 2 Chron. 18

☐ **Jun. 30** 2 Chron. 19–23

☐ **Jul. 1** Obad. 1; Ps. 82–83

☐ **Jul. 2** 2 Kings 1–4

☐ **Jul. 3** 2 Kings 5–8

☐ **Jul. 4** 2 Kings 9–11

☐ **Jul. 5** 2 Kings 12–13; 2 Chron. 24

☐ **Jul. 6** 2 Kings 14; 2 Chron. 25

☐ **Jul. 7** Jonah 1–4

☐ **Jul. 8** 2 Kings 15; 2 Chron. 26

☐ **Jul. 9** Isa. 1–4

☐ **Jul. 10** Isa. 5–8

☐ **Jul. 11** Amos 1–5

☐ **Jul. 12** Amos 6–9

☐ **Jul. 13** 2 Chron. 27; Isa. 9–12

☐ **Jul. 14** Mic. 1–7

☐ **Jul. 15** 2 Chron. 28; 2 Kings 16–17

☐ **Jul. 16** Isa. 13–17

☐ **Jul. 17** Isa. 18–22

☐ **Jul. 18** Isa. 23–27

☐ **Jul. 19** 2 Kings 18:1–8; 2 Chron. 29–31; Ps. 48

☐ **Jul. 20** Hos. 1–7

☐ **Jul. 21** Hos. 8–14

☐ **Jul. 22** Isa. 28–30

☐ **Jul. 23** Isa. 31–34

☐ **Jul. 24** Isa. 35–36

☐ **Jul. 25** Isa. 37–39; Ps. 76

☐ **Jul. 26** Isa. 40–43

☐ **Jul. 27** Isa. 44–48

☐ **Jul. 28** 2 Kings 18:9–19:37; Ps. 46; Ps. 80; Ps. 135

☐ **Jul. 29** Isa. 49–53

☐ **Jul. 30** Isa. 54–58

☐ **Jul. 31** Isa. 59–63

☐ **Aug. 1** Isa. 64–66

☐ **Aug. 2** 2 Kings 20–21

☐ **Aug. 3** 2 Chron. 32–33

☐ **Aug. 4** Nah. 1–3

☐ **Aug. 5** 2 Kings 22–23; 2 Chron. 34–35

☐ **Aug. 6** Zeph. 1–3

☐ **Aug. 7** Jer. 1–3

☐ **Aug. 8** Jer. 4–6

☐ **Aug. 9** Jer. 7–9

☐ **Aug. 10** Jer. 10–13

☐ **Aug. 11** Jer. 14–17

☐ **Aug. 12** Jer. 18–22

☐ **Aug. 13** Jer. 23–25

☐ **Aug. 14** Jer. 26–29

☐ **Aug. 15** Jer. 30–31

☐ **Aug. 16** Jer. 32–34

☐ **Aug. 17** Jer. 35–37

☐ **Aug. 18** Jer. 38–40; Ps. 74; Ps. 79
☐ **Aug. 19** 2 Kings 24–25; 2 Chron. 36
☐ **Aug. 20** Hab. 1–3
☐ **Aug. 21** Jer. 41–45
☐ **Aug. 22** Jer. 46–48
☐ **Aug. 23** Jer. 49–50
☐ **Aug. 24** Jer. 51–52
☐ **Aug. 25** Lam. 1:1–3:36
☐ **Aug. 26** Lam. 3:37–5:22
☐ **Aug. 27** Ezek. 1–4
☐ **Aug. 28** Ezek. 5–8
☐ **Aug. 29** Ezek. 9–12
☐ **Aug. 30** Ezek. 13–15
☐ **Aug. 31** Ezek. 16–17

☐ **Sept. 1** Ezek. 18–19
☐ **Sept. 2** Ezek. 20–21
☐ **Sept. 3** Ezek. 22–23
☐ **Sept. 4** Ezek. 24–27
☐ **Sept. 5** Ezek. 28–31
☐ **Sept. 6** Ezek. 32–34
☐ **Sept. 7** Ezek. 35–37
☐ **Sept. 8** Ezek. 38–39
☐ **Sept. 9** Ezek. 40–41
☐ **Sept. 10** Ezek. 42–43
☐ **Sept. 11** Ezek. 44–45
☐ **Sept. 12** Ezek. 46–48
☐ **Sept. 13** Joel 1–3
☐ **Sept. 14** Dan. 1–3
☐ **Sept. 15** Dan. 4–6
☐ **Sept. 16** Dan. 7–9
☐ **Sept. 17** Dan. 10–12
☐ **Sept. 18** Ezra 1–3
☐ **Sept. 19** Ezra 4–6; Ps. 137
☐ **Sept. 20** Hag. 1–2
☐ **Sept. 21** Zech. 1–7
☐ **Sept. 22** Zech. 8–14
☐ **Sept. 23** Est. 1–5
☐ **Sept. 24** Est. 6–10
☐ **Sept. 25** Ezra 7–10
☐ **Sept. 26** Neh. 1–5
☐ **Sept. 27** Neh. 6–7
☐ **Sept. 28** Neh. 8–10

☐ **Sept. 29** Neh. 11–13, Ps. 126
☐ **Sept. 30** Mal. 1–4

☐ **Oct. 1** Luke 1; John 1:1–14
☐ **Oct. 2** Matt. 1; Luke 2:1–38
☐ **Oct. 3** Matt. 2; Luke 2:39–52
☐ **Oct. 4** Matt. 3; Mark 1; Luke 3
☐ **Oct. 5** Matt. 4; Luke 4–5; John 1:15–51
☐ **Oct. 6** John 2–4
☐ **Oct. 7** Mark 2
☐ **Oct. 8** John 5
☐ **Oct. 9** Matt. 12:1–21; Mark 3; Luke 6
☐ **Oct. 10** Matt. 5–7
☐ **Oct. 11** Matt. 8:1–13; Luke 7
☐ **Oct. 12** Matt. 11
☐ **Oct. 13** Matt. 12:22–50; Luke 11
☐ **Oct. 14** Matt. 13; Luke 8
☐ **Oct. 15** Matt. 8:14–34; Mark 4–5
☐ **Oct. 16** Matt. 9–10
☐ **Oct. 17** Matt. 14; Mark 6; Luke 9:1–17
☐ **Oct. 18** John 6
☐ **Oct. 19** Matt. 15; Mark 7
☐ **Oct. 20** Matt. 16; Mark 8; Luke 9:18–27
☐ **Oct. 21** Matt. 17; Mark 9; Luke 9:28–62
☐ **Oct. 22** Matt. 18
☐ **Oct. 23** John 7–8
☐ **Oct. 24** John 9:1–10:21
☐ **Oct. 25** Luke 10–11; John 10:22–42
☐ **Oct. 26** Luke 12–13
☐ **Oct. 27** Luke 14–15

☐ **Oct. 28** Luke 16–17:10
☐ **Oct. 29** John 11
☐ **Oct. 30** Luke 17:11–18:14
☐ **Oct. 31** Matt. 19; Mark 10

☐ **Nov. 1** Matt. 20–21
☐ **Nov. 2** Luke 18:15–19:48
☐ **Nov. 3** Mark 11; John 12
☐ **Nov. 4** Matt. 22; Mark 12
☐ **Nov. 5** Matt. 23; Luke 20–21
☐ **Nov. 6** Mark 13
☐ **Nov. 7** Matt. 24
☐ **Nov. 8** Matt. 25
☐ **Nov. 9** Matt. 26; Mark 14
☐ **Nov. 10** Luke 22; John 13
☐ **Nov. 11** John 14–17
☐ **Nov. 12** Matt. 27; Mark 15
☐ **Nov. 13** Luke 23; John 18–19
☐ **Nov. 14** Matt. 28; Mark 16
☐ **Nov. 15** Luke 24; John 20–21
☐ **Nov. 16** Acts 1–3
☐ **Nov. 17** Acts 4–6
☐ **Nov. 18** Acts 7–8
☐ **Nov. 19** Acts 9–10
☐ **Nov. 20** Acts 11–12
☐ **Nov. 21** Acts 13–14
☐ **Nov. 22** James 1–5
☐ **Nov. 23** Acts 15–16
☐ **Nov. 24** Gal. 1–3
☐ **Nov. 25** Gal. 4–6
☐ **Nov. 26** Acts 17–18:18
☐ **Nov. 27** 1 Thess. 1–5; 2 Thess. 1–3
☐ **Nov. 28** Acts 18:19–19:41

☐ **Nov. 29** 1 Cor. 1–4
☐ **Nov. 30** 1 Cor. 5–8

☐ **Dec. 1** 1 Cor. 9–11
☐ **Dec. 2** 1 Cor. 12–14
☐ **Dec. 3** 1 Cor. 15–16
☐ **Dec. 4** 2 Cor. 1–4
☐ **Dec. 5** 2 Cor. 5–9
☐ **Dec. 6** 2 Cor. 10–13
☐ **Dec. 7** Acts 20:1–3;
    Rom. 1–3
☐ **Dec. 8** Rom. 4–7
☐ **Dec. 9** Rom. 8–10

☐ **Dec. 10** Rom. 11–13
☐ **Dec. 11** Rom. 14–16
☐ **Dec. 12** Acts
    20:4–23:35
☐ **Dec. 13** Acts 24–26
☐ **Dec. 14** Acts 27–28
☐ **Dec. 15** Col. 1–4;
    Philem. 1
☐ **Dec. 16** Eph. 1–6
☐ **Dec. 17** Phil. 1–4
☐ **Dec. 18** 1 Tim. 1–6
☐ **Dec. 19** Titus 1–3
☐ **Dec. 20** 1 Peter 1–5

☐ **Dec. 21** Heb. 1–6
☐ **Dec. 22** Heb. 7–10
☐ **Dec. 23** Heb. 11–13
☐ **Dec. 24** 2 Tim. 1–4
☐ **Dec. 25** 2 Peter 1–3;
    Jude 1
☐ **Dec. 26** 1 John 1–5
☐ **Dec. 27** 2 John 1;
    3 John 1
☐ **Dec. 28** Rev. 1–5
☐ **Dec. 29** Rev. 6–11
☐ **Dec. 30** Rev. 12–18
☐ **Dec. 31** Rev. 19–22

Appendix B

Where Can I Learn More?

Resource List by Chapters

Introduction

Keller, Timothy. *The Reason for God*. New York: Penguin Books, 2008.

Why Are There So Many Translations?

Fee, Gordon D., and Mark L. Strauss. *How to Choose a Translation for All Its Worth*. Grand Rapids, MI: Zondervan, 2008.

Fee, Gordon D., and Douglas Stuart. *How to Read the Bible for All Its Worth*. Grand Rapids, MI: Zondervan, 2009.

The Heart of the Reader

Chester, Tim. *You Can Change*. Wheaton, IL: Crossway, 2013.

Tozer, A. W. *The Pursuit of God*. Camp Hill, PA: Wing Spread Publisher, 2006.

The Gospels

Keller, Timothy. *The Gospel in Life: Grace Changes Everything.* Grand Rapids, MI: Zondervan, 2013.

Peterson, Eugene. *Tell It Slant.* Grand Rapids, MI: Eerdmans, 2008.

The Epistles

Douglas, J. D., ed. *New Bible Dictionary.* Leicester, England: Inter-Varsity Press, 1996.

Keener, Craig. *The InterVarsity Background of the New Testament.* Downers Grove, IN: InterVarsity Press, 1993.

The Old Testament Narratives

Longman III, Tremper. *An Introduction to the Old Testament.* Grand Rapids, MI: Zondervan, 2009.

Walton, John, Victor Matthews, and Mark Chavalas. *The InterVarsity Background of the Old Testament.* Downers Grove, IL: InterVarsity Press, 2000.

Poetry in the Bible

Altar, Robert. *The Wisdom Books: Job, Proverbs and Ecclesiastes.* New York: W. W. Norton, 2010.

Longman III, Temper, and Peter Enns. *Dictionary of the Old Testament: Wisdom, Poetry and Writings.* Downers Grove, IL: Inter-Varsity Press, 2008.

Spurgeon, Charles. *The Treasury of David.* Public Domain.

The Prophetic Literature

Dever, Mark. *The Message of the Old Testament.* Wheaton, IL: Crossway, 2006.

See *Longman's Dictionary of the Old Testament.*

Other Works Worth Knowing

Grudem, Wayne. *Systematic Theology*. Grand Rapids, MI: Zondervan, 2008.

Wright, N. T. *Scripture and the Authority of God: How to Read the Bible Today*. New York: Harper Collins, 2011.

How to Get a Free Bible

There are great websites that have the entire Bible (and many translations) available free of charge online. The most popular one as of this writing is www.biblegateway.com. They have more than twenty translations in English, plus more than fifty translations in other languages—all just one click away. Commentaries and other study tools are also available at this site.

If you use a smartphone, there are multiple applications that allow you to store as many translations of the Bible on your phone as its memory will allow. The YouVersion Bible is currently a very popular download.

Another wonderful option is www.freebibles.net. They will send a gently used Bible through the mail to those who need one. It is important to note that this group does not compile names to create mailing lists for any other solicitations. This may not be the optimal way to get the translation you want, but it is a great option.

The American Bible Society and the Gideons also accept requests for free Bibles for specific groups, such as hotels, prisons, hospitals, nursing homes, and others. Visit their sites at www .americanbible.org and www.gideons.org.

Notes

Introduction

1. National Endowment for the Arts, November 19, 2007, http://www.nea.gov/news/news07/TRNR.html.

2. I am fully aware that this brief account does not do justice to my conversion from atheism to Christianity and that it may cause a number of questions to arise, but I feel the subject is best left to another writing.

3. Romans 1:16

Chapter 1: Why Are There So Many Translations?

1. Though a few books have brought into question the validity of the ancient manuscripts, don't let the sensationalism fool you. The majority of scholarship maintains that the documents that we have today give us an excellent foundation for knowing what the original writings said.

2. Many thanks to Gordon Fee and Douglas Stuart for their helpful breakdown of translations in their book *How to Read the Bible for All Its Worth*. (See appendix B.)

3. Gordon Fee and Douglas Stuart, *How to Read the Bible for All Its Worth*, 2nd ed. (Grand Rapids, MI: Zondervan, 2009), 35–36.

4. It is important to note that even though the documents the King James translators used were not as accurate as the documents we have today, there were no major errors that affected doctrine or the basic thrust of the Scripture.

Chapter 2: The Heart of the Reader

1. Genesis 42:28; 1 Samuel 4:13; 2 Samuel 14:1
2. Exodus 7:23; Deuteronomy 4:9; 1 Kings 3:9
3. Mark 3:5; Ezekiel 11:19; 2 Corinthians 3:3
4. 1 Samuel 16:7; Proverbs 4:2; Ephesians 3:17
5. Genesis 1:1–3, 26–27
6. N. T. Wright, *Simply Christian* (San Francisco: HarperCollins, 2006), 181.

Chapter 3: Writing Styles in the Bible

1. Census of Marine Life, www.coml.org, September 8, 2011.
2. Environment News Service, www.ens-newswire.com/ens/oct2010 /2010–10–05–02.html, September 8, 2011.
3. Psalm 8:1
4. Francis Collins, *The Language of God* (New York: Free Press, 2006), 225.

Chapter 4: Abraham: Friend of God

1. See Joshua 24:2.
2. The first mention of Jerusalem will not occur until Joshua 10:5, long after these events have occurred. The name means "city of peace."

Chapter 5: The Gospels

1. Fee and Stuart, *How to Read the Bible for All Its Worth,* 114.
2. These texts were written by Roman historians Cornelius Tacitus and Suetonius and Jewish historian Josephus, to name a few.
3. C. S. Lewis, *Christian Reflections* (Grand Rapids, MI: Eerdmans, 1995), 155.
4. A great book that unfolds this parable is *The Prodigal God* by Timothy Keller. Highly recommended!

Chapter 6: The Epistles

1. For more information on this process, take a look at Neil R. Lightfoot, *How We Got the Bible* (Grand Rapids, MI: Baker Books, 2003).
2. *New Bible Dictionary,* 3rd ed. (Downers Grove, IL: InterVarsity Press, 1996), 393.
3. Galatians 3:28; Colossians 3:11; Philemon 16
4. Genesis 1–2

5. Genesis 3

6. Genesis 12:1–5

7. Romans 3:21–26

8. Acts 2, 11

9. 2 Corinthians 5:17

10. Romans 8:18–25

11. Revelation 21–22

12. Many thanks to Fee and Stuart for their influence on the next two guidelines. (See appendix B.)

13. Some writers attribute this quote to Saint Augustine, but others to Catholic Archbishop Marco Antonio de Dominis.

Chapter 7: The Old Testament Narratives

1. 1 Samuel 17

2. Joshua 1

3. Genesis 32:22–31

4. Genesis 12

5. Genesis 32:28

6. Edmund Clowney, *Preaching Christ in All of Scripture* (Wheaton, IL: Crossway Press, 2003), 92–93.

7. 1 Timothy 2:5

8. Matthew 5:18; Luke 16:16–17

9. Leviticus 11

10. Deuteronomy 22:9–11

11. Exodus 25:8—27:21

12. 1 Timothy 3:2

13. Genesis 37:1–36

Chapter 8: Moses: The Man Who Saw God Face-to-Face

1. Exodus 1:7 NLT

2. Genesis 28:16

3. Exodus 12:37 records 600,000 men coming out of Egypt. Scholars speculate the number to be two million, adding women and children.

4. Numbers 11:10–15

Chapter 9: Poetry in the Bible

1. In theology, there are entire categories of description about God that are called the Incommunicable Attributes. For example: He is eternal. To

talk about God's eternal nature means that we need to begin a thought, which immediately creates a gap in our understanding of a being that has no beginning.

Another attribute is that He is omnipresent, or everywhere at all times. However, we can be in only one place at a time, so we have no frame of reference for that trait. These are two aspects of God that we can't fully understand or explain.

2. Psalm 18:8–15

3. 2 Samuel 22:2–3, 32, 47

4. Isaiah 55:12

5. Psalm 18:33

6. Fee and Stuart, *How to Read the Bible for All Its Worth*, 190.

7. Acts 17:24–28

Chapter 10: David: A Man After God's Own Heart

1. 2 Samuel 22

Chapter 11: The Prophetic Literature

1. Matthew 3:1–6

2. Exodus 7:11; Mark 13:22; Matthew 24:23–24; 1 John 4:1

3. A study of Jeremiah 23:9–40 and Deuteronomy 18:10–22 will give you references on how to determine false prophets from true prophets.

4. 1 Kings 17

5. 2 Kings 2:15

6. Exodus 15:20

7. Judges 4:4

8. Acts 21:10–12

9. Matthew 21:5; John 12:15

Chapter 12: Jesus: God With Us

1. Matthew 4:23

2. 1 Corinthians 15:20–22

3. Mark 2:7

Epilogue: A Final Word

1. Genesis 1:1–3

2. This doctrine demands much more than we can explore here. Note the book references in appendix B. A few other Bible references would be

1 Peter 1:2, Philippians 2:5–11, Matthew 3:16–17, and Matthew 28:18–20. These Scriptures describe the Father, Son, and Holy Spirit as God.

3. Take some time to read the book of Hebrews. It examines the Old Testament through the lens of Christ.

4. Acts 2

5. Exodus 3:1–10

6. John 16:13–15

7. 2 Corinthians 4:4; 1 Corinthians 1:21; Romans 5:12; Jeremiah 17:9

8. Matthew 27:45–54

David Whitehead has been helping people connect with Jesus Christ for more than thirty years in churches throughout the United States and abroad. In 2009, Carl Vassar and David launched thedailybibleverse.org, which has 600,000 followers and is the number-one search result for the term *daily Bible verse* on Google. He is the lead pastor of Grace, a congregation in Manhattan, as well as a church planting coach for Acts 29 and Redeemer Presbyterian Church's City to City. David and his wife, Kathleen, live in Manhattan with their two daughters. Learn more at www.thedailybibleverse.org.

More Bible Resources

Reading the Bible can be intimidating, no matter where you are in your faith walk. In this reader-friendly guide to the whole Bible, two respected professors offer helpful book-by-book summaries that cut to the heart of the text, as well as application for what it means to you.

The Quick-Start Guide to the Whole Bible by Dr. William H. Marty and Dr. Boyd Seevers

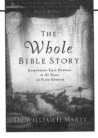

Here, you can experience the Bible in one easy-to-read chronological account. All the stories you remember from childhood are part of one grand narrative. It's the page-turning story of God's pursuit of *you*—one you'll want to read again and again.

The Whole Bible Story by Dr. William H. Marty

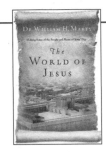

To understand Jesus' life and ministry, we need to understand the history and culture of His world. In this book, Dr. William H. Marty provides a narrative history of Israel leading up to Jesus' arrival, and connects that history to passages in the New Testament.

The World of Jesus by Dr. William H. Marty

◊BethanyHouse

Stay up-to-date on your favorite books and authors with our free e-newsletters. Sign up today at bethanyhouse.com.

Find us on Facebook. facebook.com/BHPnonfiction

Follow us on Twitter. @bethany_house